'Psychoanalysts talk of magical thinking; but what of magical seeing？？？ In this inspired volume, Dodi Goldman asks: "Can we both imagine and see things as they truly are"? Serving as psychoanalyst-docent for works of art as different as a painting from Magritte and (my favorite!) a figurine with the body of a human and head of a lion, Goldman masterfully guides the reader through complex realms of phantasy, imagination, illusion, dreaming, reality, narrative, truth and falsity. Wonders await.'

Bruce Reis, Ph.D., *North American regional editor,*
International Journal of Psychoanalysis;
IPA training & supervising analyst.

'In Dodi Goldman's *A Shimmering Landscape,* sequel to his award-winning *A Beholder's Shar*e, readers are once again welcomed on an inspiring exploration of what comes alive in the play of our imaginings – or not. His beautiful prose brings Winnicott's ideas to new life, capturing the truth that through our imaginings we come more fully to life and meaning.'

Rachael Peltz, s*upervising and personal analyst; co-director, Community Psychoanalysis Track and Consortium, Psychoanalytic Institute of Northern California, author* Activating Lifeness in the Analytic Encounter: The Ground of Being in Psychoanalysis.

'Writing with warmth and wisdom, Dodi Goldman invites us to accompany him as he draws out implications of Winnicott's views on the somatopsychic foundation of experience and of psyche as the imaginative elaboration of aliveness. In demonstrating his own creative capacity to respond to surprises, he encourages and better equips us to do likewise. This imaginative reworking of our understanding of phantasy and reality is a journey well worth taking.'

Adrian Sutton, *fellow of the Royal College of Psychiatry, U.K.; director, Squiggle Foundation, London; author* Paediatrics, Psychiatry & Psychoanalysis: through countertransference to case management.

A Shimmering Landscape

Acclaimed Winnicott scholar Dodi Goldman offers an intriguing account of the psyche's work of imaginative elaboration.

Why does the world feel one way when we are imaginatively alive to it and quite another when we are not? How does one both imagine and see things as they are? What happens when we cannot do so? This book creatively explores the interplay between the imaginative and actual in psychoanalysis and life. Each chapter centers around an evocative visual image—a prehistoric figurine, a Hindu lithograph, an Italian etching, an Inuit statue, a painting by Magritte, and more—to reveal unexpected connections and novel insights into what enlivens experience to make the personal landscape shimmer.

With a fresh and delightfully playful approach, this volume is essential reading for psychoanalysts, psychotherapists, humanities scholars, and anyone curious about the fragile alliance between the imaginative and actual in human experience.

Dodi Goldman is Training and Supervising Analyst and Faculty at the William Alanson White Institute in New York. His previous books include *In Search of the Real: The Origins and Originality of D.W. Winnicott* and *A Beholder's Share: Essays on Winnicott and the Clinical Imagination*, which won the 2017 Gradiva Award for Best Book in Psychoanalysis.

Psychoanalysis in A New Key Book Series
Donnel Stern
Series Editor

When music is played in a new key, the melody does not change, but the notes that make up the composition do: change in the context of continuity, continuity that perseveres through change. Psychoanalysis in a New Key publishes books that share the aims psychoanalysts have always had, but that approach them differently. The books in the series are not expected to advance any particular theoretical agenda, although to this date most have been written by analysts from the Interpersonal and Relational orientations.

The most important contribution of a psychoanalytic book is the communication of something that nudges the reader's grasp of clinical theory and practice in an unexpected direction. Psychoanalysis in a New Key creates a deliberate focus on innovative and unsettling clinical thinking. Because that kind of thinking is encouraged by exploration of the sometimes surprising contributions to psychoanalysis of ideas and findings from other fields, Psychoanalysis in a New Key particularly encourages interdisciplinary studies. Books in the series have married psychoanalysis with dissociation, trauma theory, sociology, and criminology. The series is open to the consideration of studies examining the relationship between psychoanalysis and any other field—for instance, biology, literary and art criticism, philosophy, systems theory, anthropology, and political theory.

But innovation also takes place within the boundaries of psychoanalysis, and Psychoanalysis in a New Key therefore also presents work that reformulates thought and practice without leaving the precincts of the field. Books in the series focus, for example, on the significance of personal values in psychoanalytic practice, on the complex interrelationship between the analyst's clinical work and personal life, on the consequences for the clinical situation when patient and analyst are from different cultures, and on the need for psychoanalysts to accept the degree to which they knowingly satisfy their own wishes during treatment hours, often to the patient's detriment.

A full list of all titles in this series is available at:
https://www.routledge.com/Psychoanalysis-in-a-New-Key-Book-Series/book-series/LEAPNKBS

A Shimmering Landscape

The Imaginative and Actual in Psychic Life

Dodi Goldman

Routledge
Taylor & Francis Group

LONDON AND NEW YORK

Designed cover image: © Courtesy of Ryan Douglas, (ryandouglasarts.com)

First published 2025
by Routledge
4 Park Square, Milton Park, Abingdon, Oxon OX14 4RN

and by Routledge
605 Third Avenue, New York, NY 10158

Routledge is an imprint of the Taylor & Francis Group, an informa business

British Library Cataloguing-in-Publication Data
A catalogue record for this book is available from the British Library

Library of Congress Cataloging-in-Publication Data
Names: Goldman, Dodi, author.
Title: A shimmering landscape : the imaginative and actual in psychic life / Dodi Goldman.
Description: Abingdon, Oxon ; New York, NY : Routledge, 2025. |
Series: Psychoanalysis in a new key |
Includes bibliographical references and index. |
Identifiers: LCCN 2024029320 (print) | LCCN 2024029321 (ebook) |
ISBN 9781032881188 (hardback) | ISBN 9781032889900 (paperback) |
ISBN 9781003536246 (ebook)
Subjects: LCSH: Psychoanalysis. | Imagination.
Classification: LCC BF173 .G595 2025 (print) | LCC BF173 (ebook) |
DDC 150.19/5–dc23/eng/20240923
LC record available at https://lccn.loc.gov/2024029320
LC ebook record available at https://lccn.loc.gov/2024029321

ISBN: 9781032881188 (hbk)
ISBN: 9781032889900 (pbk)
ISBN: 9781003536246 (ebk)

DOI: 10.4324/9781003536246

Typeset in Times New Roman
by Newgen Publishing UK

This book was written in dark times. It is dedicated to those who open space to imagine new horizons.

Contents

Acknowledgments

Writing is a solitary pursuit but by no means a solo voyage. Many ideas in this book came from elsewhere, voices both past and present intricately woven into the pages that follow. The book's images—both visual and verbal—were inspired by my psychoanalytic work with individuals who, for obvious reasons, will remain nameless.

There are no good writers without good readers. I benefitted greatly from, and am deeply grateful to, friends and colleagues who generously read evolving sections of the book. Each, in their own way, helped both set me straight and keep hope alive: Mary Brady, Peggy Crastnopol, Sharon Kofman, Suzanne Little, Rachael Peltz, Bruce Reis, Michal Rieck, Joseph Schwartz, Jim Stoeri. And, most of all, my favorite in-house wordsmith, Harriet Goldman. Sometimes, the less said, the more that is heard.

Special thanks to: Donnel Stern, the editor of the series, who never faltered in encouraging me to forge on; Ryan Douglas (ryandouglasart.com), whose painting shimmers on the cover of the book; my friend Paula Nadelstern (paulanadelstern.com) and her moving Kaleidoscope Quilts; my nephew, Yadin Goldman (yadingoldman.com), without whose generous aid in all matters graphic I would have remained hopelessly flummoxed; my niece, Eve Lenert, whose keen artistic eye helped clear a path to finding what I didn't know I was looking for; and Fran Dillon, who facilitated unexpected connections.

I am also deeply appreciative to have had opportunities to present early versions of the material in various psychoanalytic forums. My thanks to colleagues on my home turf, the William Alanson White Institute in New York; Adrian Sutton and Craig Fees, for all the fun we had preparing the Madeline Davis Memorial Lecture at the Squiggle Foundation in London; Janet Shimer, Sylvia Steinert, Janet Zuckerman, and Jack

Brewster at the Westchester Center for the Study of Psychoanalysis and Psychotherapy; Zak Mucha, Alan Levy, and Toula Kalven at the Chicago Center for Psychoanalysis; and Emily Seidel at the Psychoanalytic Institute of Northern California. Each of these engagements helped me think through what I was trying to say and how I was saying it.

Special thanks to Sarah Laycock and the docents at the Brontë Society & Brontë Parsonage Museum in Haworth; Nadine Rabovsky at the Ulm Museum in Germany; Clive Coward at the Tate; David Hannan from Dorset Fine Arts in Toronto; Ruth McCall, co-chair of the Winnicott Trust; Dan Trujillo of the Artists Rights Society; Marilyn Palmer at the Morgan Library and Museum; Dr. Adrian Plau at the Wellcome Collection; David Murphy at the Clark Art Institute; and the dedicated staff at the Queens Public Library.

Deep appreciation to my copy editor, Louise Smith, for her responsive engagement, keen eye, and valuable tutorial in the correct (British) placement of commas. And last, but certainly not least, Georgina Clutterbuck and Aakriti Aggarwal, editorial assistants at Routledge. Thank you for being there and sending all those lifelines my way.

Introduction

A Shimmering Landscape

The phrase "A Shimmering Landscape" draws upon an interview with the Pulitzer Prize-winning poet James Schuyler. Asked about his path to poetry, Schuyler said that, as an adolescent, he thought he'd become an architect despite "having no particular gift in that direction." But in the back of his house was a gully, a wilderness area where he set up a tent. Alone in his tent one summer day, he read Logan Pearsall Smith's classic memoir, *Unforgotten Years*. In the memoir, Smith describes the poet Walt Whitman sitting in the outhouse behind their home singing "Old Jim Crow" to himself. Listening to Whitman, Smith imagined maybe he, too, could someday become a writer. Reading this account, Schuyler suddenly, *"looked up from the book to the landscape outside and it all sort of shimmered."*

The interviewer then asks Schuyler: "So, has being a writer always kept that aura of phantasy … about it for you?"

"What aura of phantasy?" Schuyler replied, "It all seems very real to me."[1]

There is a divide within psychoanalysis regarding Schuyler's shimmering landscape, the world that "seems very real" when felt from within but appears as nothing but the aura of phantasy when seen from without; what Wallace Stevens once referred to as "tasting at the root of the tongue the unreal of what is real."[2] This volume engages that divide. It asks: What makes the landscape shimmer in a deeply personal way? Can we both imagine and see things as they truly are? How does one anchor riotous imaginings without undue loss of vitality? What brings our experiences to life and brings life to what we experience?

I am acutely aware how difficult it is to find words for the intimate vibrancy that makes the landscape shimmer, for how the world feels one way when we are alive to it and quite another when we are not. In fact, it is

DOI: 10.4324/9781003536246-1

so difficult to find words that I have ended up using a rather familiar one—imaginative—in a somewhat unfamiliar way. I'm hoping the reader will be willing to come along, at least part of the way, toward a novel and perhaps more radical connotation of the word.

It would probably serve us well to put aside the term "*the* imagination," for there is no such thing or substance residing in the mind. Imagining, which entails the play of psyche-soma in relation to the possibility of things, is a present continuous verb. Bodying forth from "the riot of things beyond order and form,"[3] it is an animating activity imbuing visceral experience with a sense of reality, richness, intelligibility, and meaning. Even as we are inevitably embedded in what is, imagining allows leeway to weave ourselves into what might yet be. Mere happenings become personal experiences by virtue of a primal, originary, and idiosyncratic process, which Wordsworth once called the "blood and vital juices of the mind,"[4] and for which I use the word imaginative.

Admittedly, throughout this volume, I play somewhat footloose and fancy-free with the term imaginative. Like any concept, it risks being rendered meaningless if stretched too wide or narrowed to encompass too little. Historically, the imaginative has been understood both as a representational faculty reproducing images of some pre-existing reality and as a creative faculty producing original images. While I take these conceptual distinctions seriously, I hope the reader will bear with my inclination not to take them too rigorously and will feel there is benefit to be gained by allowing—as befits the imaginative—a degree of freedom in using the term. I am less concerned with defining the imaginative precisely than with exploring the quality of experiencing related to its interplay with what is actual, the fluctuating capacity "to weave other-than-me objects into the personal pattern."[5] And in considering what happens when that interplay is curtailed, constrained, or absent.

In everyday language, the words actual and real are often used interchangeably to refer to verifiable facts that exist, even in the face of psychological resistance. They both are assumed to stand in contrast to what is imagined, intended, expected, or believed. But, I prefer to use the word actual rather than real or the phrase, "in reality." My reason for doing so is to sidestep complicated metaphysical questions regarding the nature of reality—whether it is truly knowable and how we distinguish the state of things as they are from idealistic or notional ideas of them. In addition, since psychoanalysis draws an important distinction between intrapsychic reality and external reality, I want to avoid confusion as to which is being referred to. This matter is further muddied by Lacan's use of the term "The Real" to describe a dimension of experience that cannot be captured by language or representation.

Moreover, despite centuries of philosophical and psychological exploration, there can be no precise definition of what we mean by reality. Partly, this is because there is something inherently paradoxical embedded in our usage. On the one hand, the term is used to reference material facts, evidence of which is seen as incontrovertible. From this point of view, illusions really are misguided tricks our minds play upon us. Magicians, entertainers, and scoundrels are particularly adept at exploiting this propensity.

At the same time, however, what we call reality often refers to whatever culturally constructed beliefs are dominant at any given time. Most people take for granted the dominant worldview of their time and place; it is just the way things are. Or at least until a new shared imaginative vision comes to replace it. Charles Taylor calls this shared sense of reality upon which we rely for our collective functioning the "social imaginary."[6] It is less about verifiable material facts and more a matter of social trust as to what is consensually validated and accepted to be true. There are always individuals particularly sensitive to the constructed and changeable nature of the social imaginary. Often, they are to be found among artists and idealists of all kinds. Even if well adjusted and socially adept, they feel a "mis-fit" between the prevailing worldview and how they imagine things might be. As a result, it is common for them to struggle to find their place within the reality of a given social imaginary setup.

While I see no way around these complications, I prefer to use the word actual as a commonsense term that captures the not-me world (the subjective awareness of the *externality* of a world beyond oneself) with which we form some kind of imaginative relationship. There is a dimension of life that is not a feature of our fancy; nor does it go away just because we stop believing in it. Psychoanalysis has developed its own specialized vocabulary to describe the potentially fraught acceptance of the not-me world. Freudians emphasize the need to relinquish infantile fantasies and believe that, in health, a reality principle supersedes a pleasure principle. Kleinians speak of movement from omnipotent phantasy to a recognition of the object as separate and different from the thing symbolized and the need to mourn the loss of omnipotence.[7] Winnicott, who repeatedly reminds us that reality is an "insult,"[8] invented terms such as "objects objectively perceived" and "subjective objects" to distinguish between what has and has not yet been repudiated as a not-me phenomenon.[9] In the terms used in this book, alongside imaginative investment in experience, there is, in health, also a hunger for truth and a need to know what is actual and demystify falsehoods masquerading as truth. "The truth does not change according to our ability to stomach it," says Flannery O'Connor.[10] Like it or not—and we have reasons for both—the actual puts limits on our leeway.

Much of this book came as a surprise. The initial impetus emerged from a sense that the imaginative had not been given its due within psychoanalytic theory. Winnicott's description of the psyche as an "imaginative elaboration of … aliveness"[11] struck me as carrying implications that he, himself, never elaborated. It suggests that the psyche has a capacity, independent of both external reality and Freud's canonical representations of erogenous zones, to generatively imagine, and that the imaginative plays a role in both the creation of phantasy and perceptions of the outside world. Imaginative elaboration is not simply a series of mental images. It is an ongoing visceral and deeply emotional process transforming mere "happenings" into meaningful experiences. I was convinced one needn't sacrifice hard-won discoveries about unconscious life by including a re-envisioned understanding of the imaginative.

But seeing the imaginative afresh calls into question Freud's assumption that there are two, and only two, "principles of mental functioning."[12] It entails an understanding that illusion has a developmental root in a time that precedes any distinction between fact and phantasy or between objective and subjective. Situated between hallucination and delusion, illusion is not a mixing, overlapping, or some combination of psychic contents and external reality but an uncontested state of mind in its own right and a source of vitality throughout life.

The imaginative is not another word for phantasy. Phantasy creates repetitive versions of what is already known, arresting development with the deadening effect of the familiar. Imagining, depending upon how it is used, carries the *potential* to clear a path, allowing the seemingly familiar to be seen afresh. Wayward and refractory, the imaginative can promote psychic movement to enhance one's capacity to feel, think, and generate meaning—rousing experience from the deadness of the concrete. Rather than declare: "This is how things are," the imaginative asks: "Must things be as they always are? What would it be like if it were otherwise?" At the same time, the imaginative is no guarantor of a better life. Imaginings can be used benignly but can also turn toxic, grotesque, or violent, especially when they feed on fixed phantasies.

What is more, there is a strain involved in sustaining interplay between the imaginative and actual that cannot be reduced to what psychoanalysis calls conflict between pleasure and reality. Breakdowns in the precarious interplay between the imaginative and the actual create particular difficulties in living. I suggest names for such breakdowns: Abject reality, solipsistic unreality, dissociative irreality, and degrees of denialism.

Even though I imagined writing about these themes, I had no inkling whatsoever I'd become engaged with the seemingly disparate images reproduced in this book or with ideas that flowed from them. These came to me unexpectedly. But where did they come to me *from*? Putting the question that way touches on what is at the heart of this book: Can we say whether they came from within or without? I stumbled upon these images by chance. But they "caught my attention" because of something I was already bringing to my way of looking. Receptivity implies an inner readiness, a pre-reflexive inclination toward an image or idea. We "hear and apprehend only what we already half-know," Thoreau wrote in his journals.[13]

Whatever it was I was receptive to in the images was present in my everyday work as a psychoanalyst as well. Each image in this book reminds me of particular moments with people I see in my practice. The images came alive in the consulting room, and the consulting room was enlivened by the images. The further and deeper I looked, the more resonant the images became.

The responsiveness of people outside the consulting room also mattered. I found myself in contact with people, places, and things I knew little about. When docents and curators graciously shared their passionate expertise, my interest deepened. When I received no replies or tepid responses to queries, potential openings turned into dead ends. Turns out, sustaining the fragile interplay between the imaginative and actual is facilitated or hampered by particular kinds of environments.

All told, the images in this book drew me in. I allowed them to be meaningful by imbuing them with significance. An area of overlap emerged spontaneously between emotional experiences in the consulting room, the book I was imagining, and the help I was receiving from engaged others. Gradually, an instrumental order was brought to bear, and the resonant images coalesced into chapters of this book.

This book is an imaginative elaboration of Winnicott's notion of imaginative elaboration. It is fitting, therefore, that each chapter flows from, circles around, and expands upon, an evocative image:

The moment I saw an unfinished painting of a dreamy little girl, I felt it captured something I wanted to say about the place of the imaginative in psychic life. I liked that the painting, resting on an easel, was a "work-in-progress"; it brought me into the artist's process of creating an illusion of a girl lost in her own dream world. But I didn't know what the "something" I wanted to say was until I came across a line in Virginia Woolf's novel *Orlando*. "Life is a dream," Woolf writes, "'Tis waking that kills us. He who robs us of our dreams robs us of our life."[14] I wondered: Is that true? Must a part of the person die if asked to forgo illusion? Is there a way to think about illusion other than as an escape maneuver? And what do we even mean by the slippery word illusion?

A figurine with the body of a human and head of a lion, found in a limestone cave in Germany, brought me to consider the earliest roots of imaginative life. Carbon dated to approximately 38,000 BCE, the Lion-Man of Hohlenstein-Stadel is probably as close as we will ever get to the origins of the human capacity to imaginatively move beyond the concreteness of everyday life and to create shared fictions. Meanwhile, in a parallel development, our earliest forebears underwent what the historian Carlo Ginzburg sees as a momentous cognitive leap. Actual clues detected by hunters—tracks in the mud, droppings of excrement, tufts of hair—were arranged into a narrative chain, creating an "evidential paradigm."[15] The curious matter, however, is that whatever chance reworking of neural networks allowed early *Homo sapiens* to generate narratives based on evidential details also disposed them to depart from veridicality.

A First-World-War American cartoonist's whimsical silhouettes prodded me to consider why the imaginative cannot be reduced to pattern recognition and how there are varieties of imaginative sensibilities. Being told how one *should* see the world can impinge upon an individual's imaginative investment in the world. The images led me to question the view of art as projection of inner phantasy. The artist does not simply put into the

world something residing solely within him- or herself. There is a reciprocal dialogue between inner and outer. The artist experiences something
of and in the world, which may only be recognized once a resonant form is
discovered through a pliable medium.[16]

A sketch by Winnicott, in which the boundary between mother and
infant is not clearly delineated, led me to wrestle with one of the biggest
differences among psychoanalysts: Whether they are inclined to look primarily at baby's and mother's separateness or at their embeddedness. "Baby
new to earth and sky," writes Tennyson, "has never thought that this is I."[17]
One paradoxical function of imagining may be to help discover and manage
the contours of one's emerging separateness by generating an experience
not exactly limited by our skin and not exactly the same as that which can
be verified by our sense organs. The experience of emerging as a fragile but
separate "I Am Me" is imaginatively elaborated so that we come alive in a
new way. Nevertheless, embeddedness within a boundless whole remains a
part of human experience—exhilarating and terrifying—perhaps most evident in the creative process of artists in every medium.[18]

An ornate painting of the Hindu god Rama as a child reaching out to
touch a parrot perched on his mother's wrist also took me in unexpected
directions. Rama's mother provides the setting for her child to be excitedly
curious about an object felt to be part of her. But Rama is no mere passive
recipient of his mother's ministrations. While playing, he brings an idiosyncratic spark, an imaginative vitality that works in alliance with the world's
affordances. Rama's imaginative aliveness helps his mother remain good
enough! Playing entails a particular state of mind, a return to a primary area
of experiencing that precedes any differentiation between psychic reality
and external reality. As a form of illusion, playing is not a projection of
subjective phantasy onto objective reality. It is a rich interplay between the
imaginative and actual within a singular uncontested state of mind, which
is why asking the question "Is it real or not real?" immediately explodes the
experience itself.

I had no idea when I first saw an Inuit statue of a mother carrying her
child to safety that it would bring me to wonder what we mean when we
talk about aggression. I discovered the intertwining of the aggressive and
the imaginative has a genealogy all its own, beginning with a particular
Hebrew word, "yetzer," in the opening chapters of the Book of Genesis.
While it is unlikely Winnicott was familiar with the biblical "yetzer," he
saw Klein's view of the Death Instinct as "a reassertion of the principle of

original sin."[19] Furthermore, the sheer physicality of the Inuit statue led me to appreciate the connection between early motility, aggressivity, and the imaginative.

Then came the shock aroused encountering a Magritte painting of a shrunken mature woman held aloft by a rigid, imposing child. This chilling image—originally called "Maternity," but later renamed "Spirit of Geometry"—led me to wonder about distortions in development that make a healthy alliance between the imaginative and actual difficult to sustain. It suggested what the world feels like when severe constriction in imaginative aliveness precludes the transformation of disillusionment and grievance into meaningful grief. Magritte himself had much to say about why the enchantment of surrealist art should not be conflated with the projection of unconscious phantasy. But, in also cautioning the viewer to beware of the "treachery" of images,[20] he reminds us of two distinct understandings of illusion. Magritte's image also prompted a reconsideration of what Winnicott meant by "survival" and the "use of an object."[21] In writing the paper, Winnicott was to discover he was fundamentally redescribing the nature and origin of Freud's two principles of mental functioning and, with it, the dual instinct theory.

An Italian engraving of a family gathered around a table, transfixed by a huntsman's tale, drew me to wrestle with the nature of storytelling. The image reminded me of George Eliot's claim that narrative imagination is "the nearest thing to life."[22] Are we, or need we be, virtuoso storytellers? Psychoanalysis, it turns out, has been what Alasdair MacIntyre calls an "anxious stutterer"[23] regarding narrative, with pendulum swings punctuating both the history of the profession and individual treatments. If, as James Wood suggests,[24] a story always produces more stories, when is narrative coherence—with a beginning, a middle, and an end—an impediment and when a welcome feature? If what we apprehend needs to be reimagined to even register, do fiction and non-fiction ever fully part ways? What does a story—let alone an account of a story—look like *before* there are words? And how might we think about the relationship between pain, trauma, and narrative? While storytelling is ostensibly communicative, it is no less a stay against confusion, a medium through which intolerable psychic pain is imaginatively transformed into more bearable forms of suffering.

Two of the most surprising turns this volume eventually took were the discoveries of a photograph of Lucia Joyce, the psychotic daughter of the

Irish writer James Joyce, and miniature notebooks full of fantastical tales composed by the four Brontë siblings.

Lucia Joyce lived within a highly subjective world, first in tandem with her literary father and then, for most of her life, confined to a mental hospital. James Joyce, who was highly dismissive of psychoanalysis, did not want to believe his daughter was ill. Reluctantly, however, he took her for a consultation with Carl Jung. When Jung insisted she was deeply troubled, Joyce was incredulous. "That cannot be," he reportedly replied, "she talks just like I write!"[25] The story of Joyce and his daughter raises questions about the degree of overlap between make-believe, art, genius, and madness. How might we understand that Joyce reimagined modern literature while his daughter wasted away in a mental asylum?

I first saw the Brontës' miniature books, written with painstaking precision on folded sheets of paper so tiny they could fit in the palm of one's hand, at the Morgan Library in New York. Curators at the Morgan put me in touch with docents in the parsonage in Yorkshire where the manuscripts are housed. It was from them I learned about the paracosms—spontaneously created, highly detailed imaginary private worlds—created by the siblings. The paracosms generated a sophisticated subjective reality with which each child had a deeply felt and meaningful relationship. But each of the siblings, even as they collaborated, seems to have used these fictional universes differently.

While the material and images touched upon in this book range far afield and may appear foreign to each other, I hope to convey common threads, which I believe hold them together. In my mind, they share a hidden harmony, reminiscent of Bion's "selected facts."[26] There are moments, Bion notes, in which an unconscious precipitating intuition brings seemingly unrelated phenomena together, imbuing them with coherence and meaning. I'd be pleased if readers bring their own intuitions and imaginative vitality to the pages that follow.

Chapter 1

"Life Is a Dream. 'Tis Waking That Kills Us"

I was curious to meet the 15-year-old boy who prevailed upon his parents to let him speak with a psychoanalyst. "He has been asking for quite a while, but I don't know why," his mother tells me over the phone. "Anything going on with him that is of concern to you?" I ask. "Not really," she replies, "he transferred to a new school last year but is doing alright. Probably not getting the best grades he could—he's really smart—but he has friends and seems pretty happy."

The rather poised adolescent who arrived at my office the following week had no difficulty telling me what was on his mind: "I have lots of weird dreams," he begins, "like the one I had last night." He pauses briefly, wondering if it is safe to proceed. "Tell me," is all I say before he launches into a 20-minute, vividly detailed recollection of his dream. There was a scene with him on a couch wearing headphones trying to make sense of what his parents are saying to each other, another at a party in the school cafeteria followed by a frenzied escape to Afghanistan. There were spaceships, swirl pools, an orchestral performance for which he couldn't find his instrument, and descriptions of elaborate architectural designs of various rooms. I don't interrupt as the labyrinthian tale unfolds for 20 minutes. "Quite a dream," I say as he finally emerges from his absorbed reverie. "The thing is," he excitedly continues, "I have them when I'm awake too!" "You have quite an active imagination." "That's the problem!" he replies. "What makes it a problem?" "My father gets angry; he says I'm too lost in my dreams." "Do you feel lost in them?" "Oh no! My dreams are the only place I don't feel lost."

"Illusions are to the soul," says Virginia Woolf, "what atmosphere is to the earth. Roll up that tender air and the plant dies, the colour fades. … Life is a

DOI: 10.4324/9781003536246-2

dream. 'Tis waking that kills us."[1] Is Woolf right? Must a part of the person die if asked to forgo illusion?

A great deal hinges on what is meant by the slippery word "illusion." For many, illusions are associated with misperceptions, deceptions, or errors in judgment. That is, discrepancies from discernible truth. The antidote to such liability is clearheadedness, an unflinching willingness to accept reality for what it is. But, in what follows, I lean upon an alternative sense of the word. Deceptive appearances and false beliefs, although commonplace, are not the same as the imaginative. As I hope will become clear, the imaginative is a primary force developmentally *preceding* the experiential distinction between objective fact and subjective phantasy. Eventually, it is involved in mediating between conscious and unconscious as well as between inner and outer realities. When considering this version of the imaginative, the question, "Is it real or not?" has no meaning. Only once objective and subjective perspectives become potentially, even if only partially, distinguishable do deceptions and misperceptions become salient considerations. There needs to be a more developed sense of "inside" and "outside" before the illusory becomes a hazard. Once there is a register in which objective and subjective can potentially be discerned, new questions arise: "How are inner and outer kept both separate and interrelated?" and "What happens if there is a breakdown in the fragile interplay between the actual and imaginative?"

A poem by Richard Wilbur, which draws upon the image of Moorditch, suggests what is at stake. In Shakespeare's time, Moorditch was a filthy stagnant ditch outside the city walls of London and was associated with a melancholic state of mind.

At Moorditch

"Now," said the voice of lock and window-bar,
"You must confront things as they truly are.
Open your eyes at last, and see
The desolateness of reality."

Things have," I said, "a pallid, empty look,
Like pictures in an unused coloring book."

"Now that the scales have fallen from your eyes,"
Said the sad hallways, "you must recognize
How childishly your former sight
Salted the world with glory and delight."

"This cannot be the world, "I said. "Nor will it,
Till the heart's crayon spangle and fulfill it."[2]

I sometimes imagine Wilbur's poem as a conversation between Freud and
Winnicott about the two meanings of illusion. Or between Klein and others
in the British Independent tradition about the "sad hallways" of the so-
called depressive position. Wilbur's poem prompts us to consider the interplay between the imaginative and actual and points to an inherent strain
in living distinct from what psychoanalysis describes as conflict between
pleasure and reality.

Freud was reluctant to acknowledge a place for the imaginative in psychic life. The term "imagination" holds such little cachet, it doesn't appear
in the index to the *Standard Edition*. Freud had his reasons, beginning,
perhaps, with an investment in what he felt to be his most important and
revolutionary idea: That the human mind thinks in two distinctly different
modes; that there are, in his seminal formulation, "two principles of mental
functioning." Freud's method of defining and describing these principles
set them in stark *antithesis* to one another. Primary processes are iconic
and do not proceed by argument or reasoning; they employ condensation
to fuse images and displacement by which images replace and symbolize
one another; they ignore commonsense notions of time and space as well
as obvious logical contradictions. Secondary processes, in contrast, recognize contradictions and opposites, obey rational laws of logic, and respect
the constraints of time and space. Primary processes reside in the unconscious, are "primitive" and "infantile," and characterize dreaming and neur-
otic symptom-formation. Secondary processes are utilized by the conscious
ego and thought to be more advanced, healthy, and adaptive to the realities
of the external world. In short, each principle was conceived as the mirror
opposite of the other.[3]

Freud's commitment to this categorical antithesis creates problems he,
himself, became aware of. "We must admit that the characteristic of being
unconscious begins to lose significance for us," Freud notes at one point.
"It becomes a quality ... which we are unable to make, *as we should
have hoped to do*, the basis of far-reaching and inevitable conclusions."[4]
Freud realized tidy categorical distinctions do not hold up under scrutiny.
Daydreams, with their narrative coherence and realistic elements, had to
be different than what he had posited as primary process unconscious

phantasy. Similarly, although Freud suggested that, with development, a "reality principle" supersedes the "pleasure principle," he had to concede such a static stage theory makes little sense. And arguing that "one species of thought-activity" was simply "split off" from the other and "kept free from reality testing"[5] doesn't account for the way daily life appears saturated with phantasy. There had to be some measure of continuity between conscious and unconscious. In the end, Freud seemed as pained to emphasize the continuity between these aspects of experience as he was to schematically differentiate them. "We cannot do justice to the characteristics of the mind by means of linear contours," Freud concludes. "After we have made our separations, we must allow what we have separated to merge again."[6]

Many of Freud's followers—Hans Loewald and Charles Rycroft in particular come to mind—made creative efforts to address these contradictions by rethinking the relationship between the two foundational principles. They realized the penetration of phantasy into perceptions of the world is what gives those perceptions resonance, vitality, and meaning. Provided one does not adhere too rigidly to the idea that there are two, and only two, principles of mental functioning, their work opens a space for the imaginative.

Nevertheless, the notion of the imaginative as an idiosyncratic, inventive, and refractory creation of the individual remains difficult to reconcile with Freud's overall vision, particularly regarding the origins and function of what he broadly calls phantasy.

Origin stories are important here, both the origin of Freud's discovery of phantasy and what he believed to be the origins of phantasies themselves (the German "*Phantasie*" actually means "imagination"). As early as 1897, Freud writes in a letter to Fliess that he had "gained a sure notion of the structure" of neuroses. "Everything," asserts Freud, "goes back to the *reproduction of scenes*, some of which can be arrived at directly, but others always by way of phantasies set up in front of them."[7] These phantasies—elsewhere he calls them "psychical facades"—"combine things that have been experienced and things that have been heard, past events (from the history of parents and ancestors) and things that have been seen by oneself."[8] These perceived happenings—experienced, witnessed, and overheard—*reproduced* in phantasy are, Freud hastens to add, "of course genuine."[9]

It is worth wondering why the phrase "of course" seeps into Freud's account. Is he simply emphasizing that the contents of our phantasies necessarily have their origins in actual experiences? Or is he reassuring himself that the phantasies he has discovered are not inventions of some fertile imagination, his patient's or his own? Whatever the reason, Freud insisted what is represented in mind is ultimately reducible to a simple combination of a few elements—the reproduction of scenes—already furnished by the perceptual apparatus.

Later, Freud finds himself confronted with an additional problem: Some phantasies—so-called originary ones—did not seem to have any identifiable source in the actual life of the individual. To solve this quandary, Freud downplays any spontaneous creative aspect of how images emerge and instead falls back on the proposition that they must have been phylogenetically inscribed in the memory of the species.

No less significant than the origins of phantasy life was Freud's understanding of its motive and function. Despite acknowledging that "the various phantasies, castles in the air and daydreams" are not "stereotyped or unalterable," Freud claimed that phantasies invariably "hark back to a memory of an earlier experience (usually an infantile one) in which [some] wish was fulfilled." The underlying motive "of every single phantasy," he concludes, was a constant—"a correction of unsatisfying reality."[10]

Freud was committed to a view of the psyche as tragically pursuing serial substitutions for what has actually been lost. Unable to subsist on the scanty satisfactions they can extort from reality, human beings compensate themselves with a separate mental realm of phantasy in which they continue to enjoy a measure of what they were forced to relinquish in the name of necessity. Unconscious phantasy and conscious daydreams provide a modicum of recompense by reproducing what had once afforded pleasure. But, and this is crucial, they never really create anything new.

While Freud does not clearly distinguish phantasy from the imaginative, he nevertheless suggests an imaginative analogy to describe them. Just as "nature reserves" are created in places where the "requirements of agriculture, communications and industry threaten to bring about changes in the original face of the earth which will quickly make it unrecognizable," writes Freud, the human mind sequesters off an area that "preserves its original state which everywhere else has to our regret been sacrificed to necessity." This mental reservation is "withdrawn from the reality principle." And most telling in this imaginative account is what Freud believed happens in this "reservation" or "nature reserve": "Everything," he writes, "including what is useless and even what is noxious can grow and proliferate there as it pleases."[11]

From Freud's point of view, it is a great misfortune that humans have "contrived to alternate between remaining an animal of pleasure and being once more a creature of reason."[12] Freud's hierarchy of mental functioning relegates images to a place inferior to reasoning and language; the work of psychoanalysis is to supplant primary imagistic processes with secondary mode word presentations. He assumes the archaic primary process remains unchanged over time and inaccessible to learning. And, in the never-ending quest for substitute pleasures, we rely upon the auxiliary constructions of phantasy, an edifice ultimately reducible to a few unchanging elements. Born of something akin to grief, imaginative life is "the opposite of … what is real,"[13] a mistress of error and duplicity severing us from truth. The challenge of living truthfully, therefore, is to resist the seductive power of the illusory. At the end of the day, the imaginative had to be subordinate to Reason. Or, at least in Freud's psychoanalytic imaginings, that is how it appears.

Winnicott's sensibility moved him to approach these matters differently. He claimed, without ever fully elaborating, that what we call "psyche" is, at its root, an "*imaginative elaboration of somatic parts, feelings, and functions, that is, of physical aliveness*."[14] Bodily needs gradually become ego needs as "psychology emerges out of the imaginative elaboration of physical experience."[15] From a psychoanalytic point of view, this is a rather startling statement. While Winnicott could be maddeningly elusive in his theorizing, he was also often remarkably precise in his choice of words. The words "imaginative" and "aliveness" resonate with, but do not correspond exactly to, "phantasy" and "sexuality."

Winnicott is not speaking of the earliest somatic or sexual pleasures as abandoned and relegated to phantasy. He is suggesting the psyche has a capacity, independent of both external reality and canonical representations of erogenous zones, to generatively imagine. Images and, eventually, ideas spontaneously add to and enhance somatic arousals to create a more complex, nuanced, and emergent whole. Imaginative elaborations arising from our very aliveness grant meaning to brute facts and are a source of pleasure all their own.

Winnicott gestures toward a radical implication, one he never fully acknowledges or develops: Imaginative elaboration, which is how visceral sensuous experience is first structured, is a primary adaptive force throughout life. It does not distort reality—which is how "illusion" is often construed—but authentically animates what is apprehended. The imaginative arises from a vitalizing psychic sphere that exists prior to any distinction between fact and phantasy. Rather than gradually be superseded by a reality principle, it makes responsive use of the actual to engender an ongoing experiential sense of aliveness. What makes imaginative elaboration "primary" is that it is not an expression or derivative of, nor is it motivated by, anything else. It is what the psyche does to render experience emotionally meaningful.

Imaginative elaboration is not constituted by fixed or unchanging elements, nor does it necessarily arise from or reproduce what has been perceived. Psychic life might be elucidated but is never reducible. In essence—if "essence" is the right word here, because there is no actual substance—the imaginative is a primary creative force rebellious toward determinacy. As such, the imaginative carries the potential to promote psychic movement, to enhance one's capacity to feel, think, and generate meaning—rousing experience from the deadness of the concrete.

The imaginative is hardly just a faculty for evoking images. It is what makes experiences feel *personal*. It is also what allows individuals to affiliate, cooperate, and create a social sphere. We rely upon imaginative capacities to navigate the terrain of personal intentions. Identification—stepping into the shoes of an other—requires an imaginative act. Beginning in childhood, imaginative counterfactuals are employed to reason about causal outcomes; novel possibilities—the stuff of endlessly evolving cultural artifacts—are imaginatively generated within make-believe frameworks. Without the imaginative, we would be locked into the sensory present, denied future horizons, and unable to comprehend someone else's account of an event.[16]

From the earliest registering of contingencies—"*If this ... then that*"—imaginative life evolves into a meaningful "*What if?*," a source of subjunctive moods heralding what could or would be "*If only* ...." The ungovernable and irrepressible human spirit opens up horizons and draws configurations of the fanciful and potentially realizable. Rather than declare: "This is how things are," the imaginative asks: "Must things be as they always are? What would it be like if it were otherwise?" As Ursula Le Guin puts it, the hallmark of the imaginative is: "*It doesn't have to be the way it is.*"[17]

For Winnicott, imaginative elaboration is what the psyche does. That is why transitionality is far more than merely a stage in development. It is a way of describing a remarkable human capacity, at every stage of life, "to weave other-than-me objects into the personal pattern."[18] Transitional relatedness generates a way of being alive not hemmed in by either solipsistic subjectivity or claims of objective perception. As psyche develops, dream life imaginatively weaves its way into living in the real world, and living in the real world weaves its way into dreaming. Imagining is the continuation of dream life into waking life and vice versa.

While the idea of psyche as a spontaneous imaginative force might be startling, it shouldn't surprise us that Winnicott was the one to posit it. Pearl King once remarked that Winnicott was like the knight piece in chess whose moves were always oblique and unpredictable.[19] Or, as one American analyst noted after meeting Winnicott, "it was as if he walked through every door sideways."[20]

Winnicott did walk through the psychoanalytic door sideways. An explorer in his own right, Winnicott's fate, like that of many creative innovators, was to initially raise hackles and be looked at askance. While he thought of himself as a contributor to the scientific understanding of human development, he was acutely aware of a paradox at the heart of the psychoanalytic enterprise: The moment primary process thinking is rendered in the language of secondary processes, it becomes something it is not. Freud's ego is itself cast in the mold of a scientist at work and modeled on the rationalist ideal.[21] How does one maintain a scientific attitude when engaged with the subjectively idiosyncratic phenomenon scientific thinking is always at pains to exclude?

More generally, Winnicott was troubled by how scientism and technology threatened human aliveness. Whereas Freud drew upon industrial advancement to create his metaphor of the imaginative as a "nature reserve" for "useless and noxious" detritus, Winnicott saw the analogy in reverse. Technology was potentially impinging upon the imaginative.

In the summer of 1969, as Winnicott convalesced from the near fatal illness he suffered during his third and final visit to the United States, the American moon landing captured his imagination. Taking stock of the moment, he penned a poem titled "Moon Landing," which read in part:

They say
They reached the moon
Planted a flag
a flag stiffened of course
(no gods breathe there) ...

Has anything altered?
Is this the shape of man's triumph,
the mark of man's greatness
the climax of civilization
the growing point of man's cultural life?
Is this the moment for setting up a god
who is pleased with his creative efforts?

No not for me
This is not my moon ...

This is not the moon of the magic casement,
Of the personal dream of Juliet of the balcony,
(Nurse I come)

My moon has no flag
no stiffened flag
Its life is in its active beauty
Its variable light
Its luminosity.[22]

"This is not my moon" captures Winnicott's experience of the "stiffened" American flag he had recently encountered when he presented his "Use of the Object" paper at the New York Psychoanalytic Society.[23,24] Winnicott was also clearly aware of the moon as a nearly iconic representation of illusion. His friend and colleague Charles Rycroft had read a paper before the British Society about how "moonlight represented illusion and the moon the idealized object that maintains the state of illusion."[25] So, in a deeper sense, "Moon Landing" communicates Winnicott's concern that the imaginative—whose "life is in its active beauty, its variable light" and makes Juliet's dream personal—be valued in its own right as a bridge to something vital and real.

Imagining is not another word for what psychoanalysis commonly calls unconscious phantasy. The notion of unconscious phantasy presumes *boundaries* between unconscious and conscious, inner and outer, wishes and reality. In contrast, the imaginative is prior to any differentiation between psychic reality and external reality. Its root lies in a type of experience in which the binary structure—inner/outer—does not yet figure.

Although "phantasy" has a variety of connotations across languages—the German, French, and English meanings do not correspond exactly—it generally refers to imaginary scenes or scripts distorted to a greater or lesser degree by defensive processes. In the final analysis, phantasies are seen as representing the fulfillment of unconscious wishes for prohibited things. These wishes are thought to be unsustainable if reality is perceived accurately.[26]

Whether understood as phylogenetically inscribed, the result of trauma, transmitted via the unconscious of the parents, or derived from what the child sees and hears (Freud proposed each of these origin stories at different times), phantasy creates repetitive versions of what is already known, arresting development with the deadening effect of the familiar. Imagining, depending upon how it is used, carries the *potential* to clear a path, allowing the seemingly familiar to be seen afresh. Psychoanalysis centered on phantasy is inclined to search for presumed causes of a decipherable past. The play of the imaginative, however, allows for the unpredictability of an unknown future. Whereas the notion of phantasy suggests an inevitable *conflict* between a reality principle and a pleasure principle, the imaginative generates an inherent *strain* of keeping inner and outer separate while at the same time maintaining interplay between them. We don't simply "see" an objective reality or solely invent a subjective one. Development is not achieved by simply replacing the latter with the former.

Without the imaginative, nothing would be "thinkable," let alone "believable." Whether arising from within or from without, impressions must first be imaginatively elaborated for them to become accessible and intelligible to consciousness. As Aristotle put it, "Never does the soul think without phantasm."[27]

Psychic material does not exist fully formed within an unconscious realm and then simply "migrate," *as is*, into consciousness. It must first be imaginatively elaborated to even register in consciousness with any measure of intelligibility. What psychoanalysis calls "lifting of repression" or "making the unconscious conscious" involves the imaginative.

This line of thinking—that the imaginative plays a part in the formulation of experience—is suggested in Bion's "theory of thinking." "Thinking," which for Bion always includes feeling, developed to "cope with thoughts." It is "forced upon the psyche by the pressure of thoughts and not the other way around."[28] An intolerable build-up of what Bion calls "beta elements"—"undigested" sense-impressions related to emotional experience—initiates the mind's ability to think.[29] But the raw experience of these "beta elements"—Edgar Alan Poe called them "unthought-like thoughts that are the souls of thought"[30]—cannot actually be "thought" unless first "contained," given a manageable form, by a function he calls "alpha." If we put aside Bion's quasi mathematical language and Poe's spiritual one, they both imply incipient or inchoate impressions must first be elaborated into dream material before they can be thought, felt, suffered, or even repressed.

To cope with emotional experience, we imaginatively recast one thing into another. Only when imaginatively elaborated into, and contained by, symbols—words, ideas, narratives, pictorial images, musical phrases, articulated feelings—can material in unconscious form be apprehended let alone comprehended. Unconscious material itself, in other words, is, and always remains, unconscious. But some portion can be imaginatively elaborated—"dreamt" Bion would say—after which it can be "thought." "Waking life is a dream controlled," remarked the Spanish-American philosopher George Santayana. "Sanity," he adds, "is a madness put to good uses."[31]

Among contemporary psychoanalysts, Donnel Stern similarly suggests that some "unthought-like thoughts" must undergo elaboration to be accessible to conscious thought. Stern coined the elegant and felicitous terms "formulated" and "unformulated" experience to capture the idea that the unconscious is not constituted by fully formed meanings that emerge into consciousness once repression is lifted.[32] There are, Stern argues, degrees of formulation of experience, and the formulation of experience is a "ceaseless, uncontrollable, and thoroughly unpredictable process of emergence."[33] What can potentially emerge into consciousness is a range of possible meanings determined, in Stern's view, by the interpersonal field in which the individual is embedded. Which meanings are "allowable" depends on the interpersonal context. Stern, too, sees the imaginative at play here. He defines imagination as "the willingness to consider the realization of all the unformulated possibilities that might be given explicit conscious expression."[34] Whether or not one adopts Stern's definition, it is clear from his account that a "thoroughly unpredictable" process of formulation is necessary for potential meaning to emerge.

It is not only previously unconscious material, however, that must be formulated. Perceptions derived from the external world undergo imaginative elaboration as well. Otherwise, they too would be unfathomable. Or, to put this another way: The play of psyche-soma transforms impressions arriving from the external world into perceptions. Historically, psychoanalysis claimed that phantasy readily distorts perception. Health, therefore, was understood to involve the withdrawal of illusory projections. But it may be the case that imagining is a welcome feature of perception itself. By cushioning the gap between sensation and apperception, imagining actually shields us from the overwhelming array of impressions.

Among psychoanalysts, Winnicott was unusually sensitive to the intertwining of perceiving and imagining. In one passage, Winnicott muses about the experience of looking at a clock. He might see what time it is. But it could just as easily happen that only the shapes on the clock dial register and not the time of day. Then again, he might look directly at the clock without even noticing it is there.

Winnicott suggests that, to actually see the clock, he has first to "hallucinate"—that is, see the clock as potentially present. When looking at a clock, he must "create" the clock he is looking at, even as he is "careful not to see clocks except just where I already know there is one." Well aware he is suggesting a counterintuitive process that defies commonsense logic, Winnicott nevertheless insists that perception is made possible through a prior apperceptive act. This "little experience of omnipotence" is not a retreat from or defense against an unbearable reality; it is necessary to make perceptual sense of what is actual.[35] Moreover, "thinking hallucinatorily"—conjuring imaginative possibilities—goes beyond mere noticing or apprehending. It makes possible a personally creative relationship with what is discerned.[36]

In noting the curious meshing between seeing and seeing in the mind's eye, Winnicott is squarely in the camp of the Spanish-American philosopher George Santayana who similarly claims "perception is in fact no primary phase of consciousness; it is an ulterior practical function acquired by a dream." Perceptions cannot be understood, says Santayana, unless "we regard [them] as forms of imagination happily grown significant."[37]

Winnicott also draws upon a well-established English Romantic tradition. Both Wordsworth and Coleridge highly value the imaginative and speak of an "intermediate" area between inner and outer. The mind, says Wordsworth, is "creator and receiver both/Working but in alliance with the works/Which it beholds."[38] And the imaginative is "a reconciling and mediatory power, which ... gives birth to a system of symbols."[39]

Long before Winnicott characterized potential space as an intermediate area of experiencing, Coleridge argued that some special capacity must mediate the mind's reaching out toward, while at the same time surrendering to, what is discovered. For Coleridge, the imaginative was such an "intermediate faculty." "Into the simplest seeming 'datum,'" he writes, "a constructing, forming activity from the mind has entered. And the perceiving and the forming are the same. The subject (the self) has gone into what it perceives, and what it perceives is, in this sense, itself."[40]

While it may seem odd, the view of these Romantics is remarkably compatible with what the Nobel Prize-winning neuroscientist Eric Kandel refers to as "top–down processing." Kandel contends that what is "seen" in the "mind's eye" refigures and goes dramatically beyond the image cast on the retina of the actual eye. We take crude signals and spontaneously conjure a believable picture in our mind, imaginatively sculpting ambiguous impressions into meaningful perceptions. Writes Kandel: "Because much of the sensory information that we receive ... can be interpreted in a variety of ways ... we must guess ... what is the most likely image in front of us."[41]

Like Winnicott, Kandel suggests perception is a guessing game we are generally really good at. With every look, we forecast what we believe the object of our attention is most likely to be, completing through imagining what Wordsworth calls the "something evermore about to be."[42] Our brains, claims the English neuroscientist Chris Frith, are predictive simulation machines, each perception an imaginative "construction that coincides with reality."[43]

Imaginative elaboration should not be conflated with magical thinking. The former evokes a creative relationship *with* what is actual while the later invokes omnipotent phantasy so as to *evade* the truth of one's situation. Magical thinking substitutes invented internal reality for actual external reality. It is a path of least resistance, sidestepping what is painful about the "world as it is" in favor of "the world as I would like it to be."[44] Instead of recognizing thoughts and feelings as subjective experiences, they are taken to be indisputable facts. In Freud's language, omnipotence is "the reality not of experience but of thought."[45] To the extent that such a state of mind eclipses an imaginative relationship with what is actual, the individual cannot learn from experience or grow. When magical thinking is invoked, there is a loss of capacity to differentiate dreaming and perceiving. When the imaginative is evoked, dreaming and perceiving interrelate while remaining separate.

It is possible, in other words, to suggest we maintain a curious contract between seeing and seeing-in-the-mind's-eye without venerating the irrational by subscribing to the preposterous notion that whimsy wills things into manifesting themselves.

The actual is no mere feature of our fancy, nor does it go away just because we stop believing in it. "The truth does not change according to our ability to stomach it," says Flannery O'Connor.[46] Psychoanalysis has developed its own specialized vocabulary to describe the potentially fraught acceptance of the "not-me" world. As a Freudian might put it: Under the sway of the pleasure principle we swallow what we like and spit out what we don't, whereas the reality principle challenges us to acquiesce to something disagreeable simply because it is true. Kleinians speak of a movement from omnipotent phantasy to a recognition of the object as separate and different from the thing symbolized.[47] Winnicott wrestled with what is entailed in transitions from relating to "subjective objects," to relating to "objects objectively perceived."[48]

As Bion suggests, truth is to the mind what food is to the body, and its lack leads to a kind of mental rickets.[49] The need to know the truth is why family secrets (not to mention blatant hypocrisy and self-deception) have such corrosive effects. Alongside imaginative investment in experience, there is, in health, also a hunger for truth and a need to know what is actual and to demystify falsehoods masquerading as truth. Like it or not—and we have reasons for both—the actual puts limits on our leeway. "Truth ends," says Joseph Brodsky, "where lies start."[50]

It is a mistake to conflate the imaginative with the good. Asked about literary influences growing up, the British writer Ian McEwan recalled having few books at hand. His family repeatedly relocated while his father made his way up the ranks of the British Army. McEwan's mother, meanwhile, was a creative inspiration to him: She anxiously spun elaborate scenarios detailing misfortunes waiting to befall herself and loved ones. "The writer in me is from my mother," says McEwan, "She was a great worrier, which requires an imagination."[51] In the worrier's overwrought imaginings, remote possibilities become imminent probabilities.

Imaginings can be used benignly and they can also turn toxic, grotesque, or violent, especially when they feed on fixed phantasies. Imaginative activities may be too pronounced or too pallid; feelings inordinately amplified, or life made stale in their absence. A person might fail to adequately distinguish the actual from the imaginary, genuine anxieties blurring into imaginary fears—a propensity readily exploited in politics. The often rather sudden appearance of night terrors in children may signal a developmental upsurge in imaginative capacities before they are well enough integrated into the personality as a whole. Imaginative imbalances can be catastrophic: Autistic children and people with schizophrenia show marked difficulties with spontaneous pretense. What have been described as narcissistic states of consciousness entail a blocking of free communication between imagistic and lexical modes of thought; images are untranslatable into words or vice versa. This absence of a bridge between words and images contributes to the impression that a person's feelings are not *in* his words or that, as Shelley Bach notes, he is "talking to himself, or that his words are circling endlessly and leading nowhere."[52]

Imaginative fictions can be a source of great pleasure and employed benignly to escape the pain of living—consider the outpouring of sentimentality unleashed by the death of Queen Elizabeth II and how the glamorous spectacle of the British royal family momentarily erases, not unlike negative hallucinations, a person's perception of actual problems in the world. It can be mood altering to be transported by fairy tales (and soap operas) and deeply reassuring to discover the monarchy survives destruction even after a particular monarch is deposed or dies ("the Queen is dead; long live the King!").

Far more pernicious are afflictions of the imaginative realm that sadly sap the spirit, precipitating the very disasters most feared: Willy Loman's "as if" fictional bluster and relentless self-promotion bringing destructive ruin or Madame Bovary's static and dissociated daydreams consuming her energy, draining the vital connection between living and dreaming.[53]

When fixed phantasies feed off fertile imaginings, perverse dreamscapes of vindictive cruelty, ruthless dominance, grievance, and victimhood can ensue. "The lunatic, the lover, and the poet are of imagination all compact," Shakespeare reminds us. They "have such seething brains ... one sees more devils than vast hell can hold."[54] Shakespeare has a point: In megalomanic flights of fancy, individuals display a horrifying disregard for anything limiting or evidentiary. Agitated plots are envisioned in which other people are treated as mere props. It can be like living under a spell.

The imaginative is no guarantor of a better life. It makes all the difference in the world how we bring imaginings to bear and the quality of interplay with what is actual.

Without adequate interplay between the conjured and the apprehended, external perceptions lack significance, inner experiences lack substance, social cooperation is fraught, and development cannot proceed. People differ in their capacity to sustain this interplay, how much credence they give to either their perceptions or apperceptions, the way imaginative life is or is not woven into the world's affordances.

And so a question arises: How do we cultivate and retain a capacity to imaginatively enliven reality, even as we see things for what they are? How do we find a personal way to live with what Marion Milner once referred to as the "interior vagabondage" of the imaginative,[55] when it can just as easily veer from the veridical as it can serve as a life-enhancing bridge to knowing and even altering what is actual?

Generally speaking, breakdowns in the fragile alliance between the imaginative and actual are associated with four types of difficulties in living, each of which can appear in varying mixtures and degrees.

One is to be so exclusively anchored in concrete reality as to be out of touch with the imaginative aliveness that renders facts personally meaningful. There can be such constriction of the imaginative that experience becomes subsumed by a wretched acquiescence to demands felt as coming from the outside. The person may be perceived as always "working hard" or "accomplishing much" because their life is spent collecting demands and obligations so as to ward off the threatening unpredictability of the personally imaginative. They fear what their imaginings communicate to themselves about their own desires. Yet by banishing the imaginative, the person's subjective experience is that life feels abject, sterile, and futile because agency and a sense of aliveness have been disclaimed.

Troublesome in a different way is the solipsism of feeding only off of oneself, disposed to the pretense that what one imagines is the same as what is actual. There is a disregard for what is limiting, evidentiary, or consensually validated. Making a go of everyday life becomes rather difficult. This may show up as relatively benign eccentric preoccupations that to others appear simply "odd." But it also can manifest in far more malignant forms. Certain individuals suffer such severe disillusionment with what the world has to offer they cannot find any value in things as they actually are. Instead, they live with the fictive belief that their own imaginings are all that really matter. Some become solipsistic mental predators who forcefully impose their personal version of "reality" upon others, compelling them through charisma or coercion to accept whatever they, at any given moment, deem to be true. The mental predator's unmoored imaginative world can overwhelm other people's capacity to discern for themselves what is actual. Finally, in extreme cases of solipsistic withdrawal, alive interplay between the imaginative and actual is replaced by chaotic bizarreness and flagrant psychosis. To be solipsistically enclosed is to be lost in an active but isolated tyranny of self-consideration.

A constriction of interplay between the imaginative and actual is also a hallmark of dissociative disconnect. In trauma, awake dreaming and perceiving oscillate rather than interrelate. A vigilantly sustained unwillingness to allow free leeway between the two creates a dreamlike sense of observing oneself from outside one's own body and a hazy perception of the external world. While, from a more objective point of view, an abusive situation may be observed to frequently recur, the individual relates each time anew with profound disbelief—what is happening isn't "really" happening despite it having happened many times before. The external world thus becomes eerily "irreal." States of dissociative disconnect are a common feature of severe post-traumatic stress. Instead of an emotionally rich elaboration of experience, concrete memories recur as flashbacks. The individual is possessed by, rather than in possession of, their experiences. Trapped in the literal, no use can be made of the imaginative. Dissociative breakdown of interplay may entail desperate searches for stimulant forces—courting danger, compulsive excitements, and manic-like restlessness. There is much frenetic activity but little genuine vitality.

Finally, to avoid a psychologically uncomfortable truth, a more or less willful choice is made to deny or sidestep what is actual. Inconvenient truths are ignored rather than imaginatively engaged. Willful denial can coincide with a stubborn belief that one can impose one's will to bring a different reality into existence. While this may fleetingly provide a sense of triumph, there is no lasting sense of accomplishment. Prickly inflated pridefulness replaces genuine pride. Whereas denial often takes a costly personal toll, denialism, an ideological position whereby one systematically and actively refuses the truth of what is actual, has catastrophic social consequences.[56] In denialism, immediate factual reality is contested by whole groups of people who are not psychotic. Contemporary media platforms generate and exploit what Renée DiResta calls "a dissensus of bespoke pseudo-realities" in which denying and belonging go hand in hand.[57] "Pseudo-realities" are proliferating at a scale, scope, and speed never before seen. Groups cohere around dominant figures to whom entranced individuals are emotionally bound. They feel part of a select, enlightened, and cherished group in possession of a "truth," which no amount of evidence can shake. The leader "owns" reality while the actual is denied.[58]

While by no means mutually exclusive, the appearance of any of these—abject reality, solipsistic unreality, dissociative irreality, and degrees of denialism—signals a breakdown in the personally meaningful interplay between the imaginative and the actual.

Fortunately, somewhere beyond the literalness required for mere survival, sterility of solipsistic phantasies, escapism of dissociative daydreams, and the willful blindness of denialism lie opportunities to employ imaginative capacities to envisage new beginnings and better endings. Armed with imaginative capacities, we nervously or boldly step over the edge of permissible thought. Children engage in pretense, and adults are drawn to fiction—including renderings of misery—because we all seek opportunities to generate vivid imaginings. By imaginatively blending vision and judgement in due measure, we may very well—to borrow R.P. Blackmur's felicitous phrase—"add to the stock of available reality."[59]

Chapter 2

Lion-Man

The erect body is human; the head that of a lion, perhaps a lioness. It is hard to say whether this 11-inch-tall hybrid figurine carved from mammoth ivory is anthropomorphic or zoomorphic, an animal represented in human terms or vice versa. Carbon dated to approximately 38,000 BCE, it is the oldest known creature carving in the world.[1]

Its head looks directly at us. Behind the ear, a furrow is delicately carved where muscles contract when the ear turns to listen. This is not a human being hidden behind a mask. It is an imagined being gazing at and listening to us. One of the earliest examples of art and probably of religion, it gives physical form to something never actually seen but that had nevertheless taken hold in someone's mind.

Uncovered in a chamber almost 100 feet from the entrance of a cave on a limestone cliff in southwest Germany in 1939, the so-called Lion-Man of Hohlenstein-Stadel was painstakingly reconstructed from over 200 fragments. Work was interrupted because of the Second World War, but researchers returned as soon as it was feasible to do so. They could not rest until the figure was reconstructed from all the bits.

Given the technical mastery and tools available at the time, experts estimate it probably took whoever created the figurine about 400 hours of work. Digital microscope analysis reveals traces of an organic substance, presumed to be blood, inside the mouth. Intriguingly, the natural irregularities usually found on the surface of mammoth ivory have all been smoothed away, suggesting this figure was passed around from person to person over many years, perhaps generations.

When asked why any group struggling to survive in such precarious conditions would allow an individual so much time off from subsistence tasks, Jill Cook, curator of Paleolithic collections at the British Museum,

DOI: 10.4324/9781003536246-3

said she did not believe it was about the hunter's connection to animals so much as "a relationship to things unseen, to the vital forces of nature, that you need to perhaps propitiate, perhaps connect to, in order to ensure your successful life."[2]

Human activity, Cook implies, has never been just a food gathering or survival strategy. Even for our earliest forebears it was intrinsically symbolic and communicative. "Every move is at the same time a gesture," says Susanne Langer.[3] Non-biological activities—art, religion, dreaming—arise from a basic human need to imaginatively communicate. As Cook suggests, a successful life gestures toward a sphere beyond instinctual impulses and physical survival.

One wonders what it felt like for our early forebears to gaze upon or touch the chimeric figure. How different it must have felt in a time before human senses were inundated, as they are today, with images everywhere. Perhaps the lion was a fetish object, in the anthropological sense of the term, casting a charm or spell. Did it offer protection, healing, divination? Or maybe it was a totem, binding the group together in pledged solidarity. Was the lion felt to be an ancestor? Did the huntsman identify with the lion as ferocious predator? Or did the lion's gaze remind him he was liable to be the lion's prey? There is no way to know how separate the huntsman felt from the animal world. At what point did early humans see themselves, as Freud's questionable evolutionary narrative implies, as "the animal that must not identify as such?"[4,5] We can only imagine. The Lion-Man is ripe for projections. Whatever the figure may have meant to them, this object is probably as close as we will ever get to the origins of the capacity to imaginatively move beyond the concreteness of everyday life. And it suggests that believing and belonging have always gone together. How fitting that the word chimera, which originally denoted any mythical or fictional creature with parts taken from various animals, has come to connote the wildly imaginative.

In a parallel development, somewhere between 70,000 and 30,000 years ago, our human forebears began pursuing quarry with what the historian Carlo Ginzburg calls an "evidential paradigm."[6] By arranging clues they detected into a narrative chain, hunters acquired a new grasp of causal relations in the world. They learned to reconstruct shapes and movements of prey from "tracks in the mud, broken branches, droppings of excrement, tufts of hair, entangled feathers, stagnating odors." Sometimes with urgent speed, in the depth of a forest or in a prairie they "learned to sniff out, record, interpret, and classify such infinitesimal traces as trails of spittle." These "infinitesimal traces" were then "arranged ... in such a way as to produce a narrative sequence, which could be expressed most simply as 'someone passed this way.'"[7] Ginzburg sees the evidential paradigm, deciphering actual details and linking them into a narrative arc, as a momentous cognitive leap that both guaranteed survival and lies at the inception of narrative itself, transforming facts into compelling lore.

In Ginzburg's account, the evidential paradigm eventually becomes the foundation of modern science, including psychoanalysis. Galileo's observational astronomy, Darwin's investigation of puzzling distributions of wildlife and fossils, and Freud's detailed case method, all rely on narrative organization of actual evidence as the foundation of their explanations.

The curious matter, however, is that whatever chance reworking of neural networks allowed early *Homo sapiens* to generate narratives based on evidential details also disposed them to depart from veridicality. The same narrative arc underlying the evidential paradigm is at the heart of every story, "tall tale," and piece of literature.[8,9] "Imagination begins with our first lie," says the Irish author Dermot Healy.[10] No one is sure what caused this to happen in the brains of *Homo sapiens* rather than in any of our hominin siblings.[11] An explosion of symbol forming capacities sparked new forms of communication: A limited number of sounds was transformed into an extraordinarily supple language. This imaginative use of symbols not only facilitated the transmission of actual information about dangers and pleasures in the external world: It was employed to invent imaginary creatures and make-believe situations. Our ancestors took seriously images absent from the senses but present in the mind. They acquired the unprecedented capacity to imagine—that is, to picture to themselves and to communicate things they never saw, touched, or smelled.

As the hybrid Lion-Man demonstrates, humans are endowed with the uncanny capacity to conjure and collectively share meaningful fictions. These shared figments of our fertile imaginations are not lies. Lying subverts trust. Imagined reality, on the other hand, potentially becomes consensual reality—something most everyone believes in. Rather than undermining trust, shared imaginings allow flexible cooperation and affiliations among increasingly large numbers of people, thereby exerting an actual force in the world. The Lion-Man as totem and fetish illustrates what Charles Taylor calls "the social imaginary," the imagined ideas, practices, orientations, and values necessary for social life to cohere.[12] Without shared imaginings, humans would not dedicate themselves to religion's costly commitment to counterintuitive worlds governed by supernatural agents; affiliate and cohere into ethnic, political, and professional groups; set up governments; or entertain the meaningful fictions that individuals are "endowed with rights" or that money has inherent value. Nor would our personal pain and suffering ever be shareable using words.

If we were to speculate—and, of course, what can we do other than speculate?—a guess would be that humans conjured images long before they learned to speak. If this is so, then it is likely not only that images, recollected and invented, preceded language in the development of human mentation but that wordless imagery remains a distinct mode of representation and a primary substrate of what we call "thinking."[13,14,15]

There is good reason to believe, although how this comes about is far from understood, that these spontaneously generated images are connected to the sensory-motor arousals of our "embodied minds."[16] Language, as it emerges, builds upon these foundations. "I can still remember the liquid feel of those words for rain," writes Dermot Healy about his first attempt writing about rain. "How the beads were blown against a windowpane, and glistened there and ran. The words for rain were better than the rain itself."[17]

It is no coincidence one finds onomatopoeia—words imitating natural sounds—at the root of speech. The seemingly endless permutations of language conceal an entire genealogy of affective sense perceptions imaginatively elaborated into words. A vocal gesture is a "truncated act," says George Herbert Mead; language is derived action.[18]

The psychoanalyst Ella Freeman Sharpe argues that speech fuses sense experience and thought; it is a displacement from the physical to the psychical. As such, language always conceals as much as it reveals. "In psychoanalytical treatment," says Sharpe, "our task is often that of getting through barrages of words to the sense experience and the associated thoughts." Because the child acquires the power of speech at the same time as gaining sphincter control, claims Sharpe, "the activity of speaking is substituted for the physical activity now restricted at other openings of the body." Words, Sharpe believes, are substitutes for newly controlled bodily promptings. It is only secondarily that speech "becomes a way of expressing, discharging ideas." Every "live metaphor reveals a past forgotten experience ... originally a psycho-physical one."[19]

One needn't necessarily subscribe to Sharpe's focus on specific eroto-genic zones to appreciate how language comes alive only when infused with its original bodily root. Without this vital connection, words are—to borrow a metaphor—nothing but dead letters. As Hans Loewald notes, well before semantic meanings can be apprehended, an infant is "embedded in a flow of speech that is part and parcel of a global experience within the mother–child field."[20] The child is bathed in mother's speech as part of the sensual lived world. Even as a child comes to grasp nuanced semantic meanings, "the emotional relationship to the person from whom the word is learned" continues to play "a significant ... part in how alive the link between thing and word turns out to be."[21] For Loewald, words conjure their sensory-motor histories, and the interpersonal world in which the child is embedded animates the connection between words and what they signify.[22] Although Loewald adheres to the framework of Freud's two principles of mental functioning, a consistent theme in his writing is that what brings vitality to life is the reconnection of differentiated structures with their earlier origins. As Paul Valéry says, language "enjoins upon us to come into being much more than it stimulates us to understand."[23]

Both Sharpe and Loewald remind us that language is permeated with early sensuous experiences and relationships. When there is an imaginative connection with the intensities of early aliveness, words become more than "just words." They carry a charge well beyond their concrete signification. Like the landscape, words can shimmer, which is why highly sophisticated large language model AI programs might competently *simulate* language, but people are *moved* by words.

What Winnicott adds to this account is the idea that, no matter how rich the linkage between words and their sensuous origins, words are testi-mony to a degree of separation between mother and baby.[24] Winnicott may have been influenced by Sharpe when he suggests that "infants become masters at various techniques for *indirect communication*, the most obvious of which is language."[25] These "techniques for indirect communication" become necessary as baby gradually transitions from a world of direct com-munication with mother as an imaginatively conjured "subjective object" to one in which she is apprehended more objectively.

Even as we are enriched by language, we are reminded of the loss inherent in the need to use words in the actual world. Because the feelings of separateness associated with having to use words include a degree of emotional violence, Lacan calls language "the murder of the thing."[26] At the same time, words carry the potential for a rich exchange between inner and outer. Language is a potential bridge between the imaginative and the actual.

And the bridge goes both ways, for language is a Janus-faced creature, looking both outside in and inside out. As Bakhtin says, language belongs first to others, "populated" with their meanings and intentions.[27] As it is acquired, language can be made more or less one's own. But it is never *only* one's own, which is why it is worth wondering when a person is really speaking as and for themselves.

Early imaginative elaboration of physical functioning evolves into a metaphoric mapping of bodily experience onto verbal abstract concepts. Language is saturated with metaphor—I "fall" in love; I "grasp" what you mean; I'm "weighed down" or "jump for joy"; I feel like I'm "leaking," "torn asunder," or "going over the edge." These imaginative metaphors—establishing relationships between dissimilar domains—are not mere embellishments of speech. They use mental imagery from sensorimotor domains to give form to ambiguous and amorphous feeling states.[28]

The groundbreaking cognitive psychologist Amos Tversky believes there are good reasons to be suspicious of metaphors. He sees them as weak substitutes for thinking. Because metaphors are compelling, memorable, and difficult to analyze rationally, they impact human judgment even when they are inappropriate or misleading. Metaphors substitute semantic ambiguity for genuine uncertainty about the world. A metaphor, Tversky concludes, is a "cover up."[29]

Tversky has a point. Metaphors matter profoundly. And when they function unreflectively they can seduce us into not looking any deeper. At the same time, however, it is hard to escape the irony that Tversky employs a metaphor—"cover up"—to voice his distrust of metaphor. Psychoanalysis, of course, has much to say about "cover ups" and seductions. To make matters worse, what Tversky says regarding the impact of metaphor on human judgment is equally true of narrative frames. The same survival skill identified in Ginzburg's "evidential paradigm"—primordial huntsmen arranging clues into a narrative chain—leaves us susceptible to being led astray by seemingly convincing stories, including our own. We are readily seduced, says Peter Brooks, by stories.[30]

Tversky may have a point, but he elides recognition that in human communication there is an ever-present tension between what words concretely denote and what they imaginatively connote. Metaphors are not just substitutes for thinking, and "thinking" is not equivalent to rational analysis. "Unless you are at home in the metaphor," Robert Frost once remarked, "… you are not safe anywhere."[31] Deep expression withers either by words being reduced to their literal referents or, conversely, when personal meaning dissipates through an excess of connotations. Expressing everything at once is the same as expressing nothing. The Israeli poet Yehuda Amichai says metaphor is "the great human revolution, at least on a par with the invention of the wheel … Metaphor is a weapon in the hand-to-hand struggle with reality."[32]

Take, as an example, a short poem Carl Sandburg penned walking along Chicago's Grant Park:

The fog comes
on little cat feet.
It sits looking
over harbor and city
on silent haunches
and then moves on.[33]

What do felines have to do with fog? There is no obvious or pertinent relationship between the two. Taken literally, this poem becomes either a nonsensical weather report or a psychotic vision. But, if one "embraces the figure of speech,"[34] allowing the confluence of denotations and connotations to simply be, an uncanny resemblance between far-flung domains is unexpectedly apprehended. The metaphor creates what Paul Ricoeur calls "a sort of shock between different semantic fields."[35] Something unforeseen, beyond the literal referents—cat and fog—emerges and reverberates. As potential space opens for generative experience, it surprisingly makes sense to see the fog perched on silent haunches. This can only happen, however, if the tensions between similarity and difference—the ways the cat and fog are and are not alike—are held in play. The power of this metaphor is not derived from a recovered memory trace, a faded perception of something we once encountered, or from a causal chain of associations. It is from the apperception of emergent meaning.

Ogden calls this "dream thinking" and believes it to be the "most profound form of thinking"[36] because it "allows us to enter into a rich, non-linear set of unconscious conversations with ourselves about our lived experience."[37] Viewing emotional experience from multiple vantage points promotes genuine psychological growth.

There is no easy cure for metaphor blindness. Because psychic growth cannot proceed without these "rich conversations with ourselves," psychoanalysis requires a language that works more by evoking than explaining. It is a language, in Danielle Quinodoz's rendering, "that is close to poetry, and centered on affects ... and conveys a synthetic rather than linear form of thought."[38] The challenge of psychoanalysis is to find "words that touch"— in the varied meanings of physical sensation, emotional resonance, and human connection.

But herein lies an irresolvable paradox: Words, a form of indirect (symbolic) communication, are relied upon to convey resonant immediacy. Even when the "right" words are found, they do not directly communicate experience but, rather, something of what experience feels *like*. The present moment has passed, but words are tasked with bringing it back to life; it is like resurrecting the dead even in the act of mourning them. Furthermore, even if imaginative metaphors aptly communicate what an experience is like, they inevitably break down. Why is it that words so readily lose their vitality? What is it that keeps the metaphor itself alive? "It is touch and go with the metaphor," says Robert Frost, "and until you have lived with it long enough, you don't know ... how much you can get out of it and when it will cease to yield ... It is as life itself."[39]

So, too, with the Lion-Man of Hohlenstein-Stadel. A small band of early humans may have survived by employing Ginzburg's evidential paradigm, but they were enlivened by a figurine that gestured beyond the concreteness of their existence. The Lion-Man stood for something, meant something, shimmered in their minds. We don't know if they had a word for the Lion-Man, but it certainly spoke to them. Until it no longer did.

WEARY AND HEAVY LADEN

GOODBYE SUMMER

Chapter 3

Night Tree Silhouettes

Despite the etymological connection to the earlier Latin verb *imitari*—to imitate, which is also the root of *imago*—imagining is actually a spontaneous and inventive antidote to mere caricature or stereotypy. Rather than producing replicas or recycling what is already known, imagining is akin to what Paul Pruyser calls *evocation*—a surprising summoning, calling, or conjuring up. "Evocation," writes Pruyser,

> pertains to such possibilities as eliciting sorrow or languor by the stimulus of a picture of a tree with drooping leaves; of musical tones producing a feeling of relief after a thunderstorm, as in Beethoven's Pastoral Symphony; of producing an apprehensive mood by intoning "Once upon a midnight dreary …"[1]

For Pruyser, evocation "involves images, but does not require imitation."[2]

A series of drawings by the American satirist Arthur Henry Young (1866–1943) illustrate how images evoke. Young originally rose to prominence drawing political cartoons decrying capitalism, war, racism, and the mistreatment of vulnerable people, which appeared in the socialist monthly magazine *The Masses*. He was twice put on trial under the Espionage Act for his opposition to military enlistment during the First World War. Later in life, Young's imaginative eye turned toward a very different subject matter—silhouettes of trees at night. Using pen and ink, he created a series of haunting portraits of trees with humanlike features, first published in the *Saturday Evening Post* and eventually collected into a volume entitled, *Trees at Night*.

On one level, Young's ink-drawn silhouettes can be seen as a natural extension of the common illusory phenomenon known as pareidolia, where random or accidental patterns of shapes and lines are seen as a recognizable image. Patterns bring satisfaction, reassurance, pleasure. From the smallest

DOI: 10.4324/9781003536246-4

of slivers up to the grandest scale, humans seek and detect patterns in and behind the events of the world. These patterns can be imaginatively turned into coherent, if not necessarily true, narratives regarding our place in the universe.

Often referred to as "seeing faces in the clouds," pareidolia is but one example of the mind's basic propensity to seek pattern recognition, particularly of the human face. Brain scans reveal that within hours of birth a baby's gaze is drawn to faces. Researchers disagree, however, as to whether face discrimination itself is innate or if there is only an inborn neural scaffolding upon which repeated exposure to faces builds.[3]

Either way, a strong argument can be made for the evolutionary advantage of facial detection. "As soon as the infant can see," writes Carl Sagan, "it recognizes faces." A million years ago, those infants unable to recognize a face "smiled back less, were less likely to win the hearts of their parents, and less likely to prosper."[4]

When Sagan writes of infants prospering, he has in mind the physical survival of the species. But, to genuinely thrive, infants need far more than what is required for physical survival. Faces of caretakers are beacons of human relatedness. The infant "drinks in the feelings of his mother's eye"[5] no less than the milk flowing from her breast. What is felt in the mother's eyes makes all the difference in the world. It can cause the landscape to shimmer by animating the infant's nascent capacity to experience "something beyond" the mere concreteness of physical sensation. With this comes a vibrant sense of being alive in the world. In contrast, an infant who fails to "win the hearts of their parents" may very well survive physically, but their emotional experience of aliveness will be sorely compromised. Pattern recognition alone is no guarantee of responsiveness.

In fact, one needn't even be human to extract a face from a clutter of detail. Facial recognition computer software can be quite proficient at culling a mass of visual cues to identify features that line up to facial patterns. But skillful pattern recognition isn't genuinely imaginative. It is easy to forget that artificial intelligence is, after all, a mimicry machine, mirroring back cumulative data amassed by humans that then feels uncannily lifelike. Replication of this sort can become a grotesque mockery of what it is to be human.

At best, the visual illusions generated by pareidolia—and other so-called "tricks" our minds play on us—are impoverished versions of the imaginative, akin to what Coleridge refers to as "Fancy." Fancy merely recycles or, in Coleridge's words, "aggregates fixities and definites."[6] But what affords the imaginative a "higher worth" is its power to create affectively rich symbols that transform the "inanimate cold world" of brute reality:

> And would we aught behold, of higher worth
> Than that inanimate cold world allowed
> To the poor loveless ever-anxious crowd,
> Ah! From the soul itself must issue forth
> A light, a glory, a fair luminous cloud
> Enveloping the Earth.[7]

Extrapolating from patterns and generating visual illusions is also a far cry from Wordsworth's description of the imaginative as "the nurse … the guide, the guardian of his heart" and "soul of all his moral being."[8] For Wordsworth, the imaginative is a "godlike faculty," enlivening all perception:

> There is creation in the eye,
> … Not less in all the other senses; powers
> They are that colour, model, and combine
> The things perceived with such an absolute
> Essential energy that we may say
> That these most godlike faculties of ours
> At one and the same moment are the mind
> And the mind's minister.[9]

Young's images, half created, half perceived, emerge spontaneously in the to-and-fro between the imaginative and actual, seeing and seeing in the mind's eye. The silhouettes neither simply replicate what is actual nor mistake a pattern resemblance for something it is not.

The iconic American photographer Ansel Adams testifies to how imagining is more evocation than replication. "When I am ready to make a photograph," writes Adams, "I think what I see in my mind's eye is something that is not literally there. What I am interested in expressing is something … built up from within rather than something extracted from without."[10] Adams does not simply *take* pictures; he *makes* them. He claims to "revisualize" what he apprehends to "make it look how it feels." Photography, Adams concludes, "is not the duplication of visual reality. ... All my photographs are photographs of myself."[11]

An art object, Adams suggests, is no mere replication. It is an object imaginatively transformed so as to hold something of both object and subject. As Anaïs Nin, an erotic adventurer who dabbled in psychoanalysis, remarked, "We do not see things as they are, we see them as we are."[12]

The British analyst Kenneth Wright makes a similar observation. Gazing at Cézanne's painting of Mont St. Victoire, Wright clearly recognizes the actual limestone mountain in the south of France. "But," he writes, "I see it through the prism of Cézanne's imagination—it has become Cézanne's mountain, the world according to Cézanne." The objective landscape has been imaginatively recreated. "In this sense," says Wright, "landscape painting is a landscape of the heart as much as a landscape of the world."[13]

Artists, it seems, are particularly sensitive to this delicate play of heart and world. They seamlessly "slip"—if that's the right word—between the actual and imaginative. "Y'know the real world," the Dutch American painter Willem de Kooning says, "this so-called real world, is just something you put up with, like everybody else." Describing his experience painting, he notes,

> I'm in my element when I am a little bit out of this world: then I'm in the real world. I'm on the beam. Because when I'm falling I'm doing all right, when I'm slipping, I say, hey, this is interesting! It's when I'm standing upright that bothers me: I'm not doing so good, I'm stiff. As a matter of fact, I'm really slipping, most of the time.[14]

For de Kooning, art is a way of coping with his extreme sensitivity to aliveness—what Virginia Woolf calls the artist's "shock-receiving capacity."[15] A wellspring of art, de Kooning implies, is the honest encounter with the vulnerability that comes when we are moved, when something outside stirs deeply within us, throwing us off balance. Imaginative aliveness entails excitement and an edging toward a loss of control. The world as it is calls forth something imaginative in us that in turn calls forth something in the world. Reality testing may allow us to distinguish and detect. But a *sense of reality* is constituted through belief in what is imaginatively called forth—each beholder's share.[16] Creative living entails remaining a bit off-center. Humans are delicately poised between an urge to discover and a need to create, a drive to discern and a capacity to imaginatively fashion what is found.

Young's silhouettes, Adams' photographs, and the paintings of Cézanne and de Kooning all conjure something new by creating and evoking what the philosopher of art Susanne Langer calls "forms for human feelings." Langer's theory of art is simple, yet profound: No matter the medium, "Art is the creation of forms symbolic of human feeling."[17] In a beautiful gloss on Langer's theory, Kenneth Wright notes that it is as if the artist says to the world: "I have felt you, world—the rhythm and pulse of your life—and am singing it and giving back to you the way you live in me."[18] Without explicitly saying so, Wright's gloss challenges the view of art as projection of inner phantasy. The artist does not simply put into the world something residing solely within themself. Art is created through a reciprocal dialogue between inner and outer. The artist experiences something of and in the world, which may only be recognized once a resonating form is discovered through a pliable medium.[19] The artist's preferred medium allows itself to be transformed as the artist imaginatively elaborates what they find in themself through the very forms being created. This imaginative elaboration of non-verbal symbols renders emotional life in a form that, Wright notes, "enables apprehension of its being rather than comprehension of its meaning."[20] The reciprocal dialogue enlivens both the artist and an otherwise mute world. Artistic creation draws back the curtain on an inherent human struggle: How does one make external reality something of and for oneself?

The way one answers that question reveals a personal aesthetic or sensibility. Sensibility is close to, but not quite, ineffable. "Any sensibility which can be crammed into the mold of a system, or handled with the rough tools of proof," Sontag notes, "is no longer a sensibility at all. It has hardened into an idea."[21] And yet, sensibility, or what Sontag also calls "taste," not only plays a part in our mysterious reactions to people and to works of art but, in her words, "governs every free—as opposed to rote—human response. Nothing is more decisive."[22]

Sensibility is not *what* we think but *how* we orient ourselves in the world. Sensibility captures our responsiveness to things—what moves or deters us; what draws our eye or shuts our hearts; our peculiar susceptibility to pleasurable or painful impressions; the kinds of feelings we are prone to have when we encounter a picture, a word, another person, a thought. These habits of mind are quite particular and orient us. They generally coalesce to form a more or less coherent personal idiom, which is why we often can identify an author we love after reading just a few lines. Even how one holds a particular theory—lightly, tightly, dogmatically, dearly—is a matter of personal sensibility. A person's imaginative sensibility may incline in the direction of the conventional or careen toward the eccentric. It may tether itself more or less tightly to the veridical or fantastical. To each their own.

Arthur Young's night tree silhouettes display a sensibility carried over from his early years as an ideologically committed illustrator. His renderings are imaginatively compelling. They help us see something in a new way, as if a surprising apparition has emerged spontaneously from within a familiar object. But Young's sensibility is not of the romantic ilk of Wordsworth and Coleridge. As the eye roams over the visual field, Young impinges somewhat on the viewers' freedom to make of the image whatever they want. By introducing a written label, Young tells us what to think and what to experience: This is "weary and heavy laden"; that is "goodbye summer." He is inclined to instruct. The night silhouettes, like his earlier political cartoons, make statements more than they raise questions.

Asked to explain their innovative work to a baffled public, Mark Rothko and other abstract expressionist painters issued a manifesto. "Make the spectator see the world our way, not his way," it declared.[23] Art can do that, helping us see the world afresh. But herein lies a risk: One person's imaginative vision can all too easily foreclose another person's imaginative elaboration. Being told how one should see the world impinges on one's own imaginative investment in the world, leaving little room for ambiguity, let alone ambivalence. Perhaps this is a shadow legacy of the readiness to recognize a human face Sagan identified as our earliest strategy for survival in the actual world. What helps the infant "win the hearts of their parents" also leaves the individual prone to adopting their caretaker's vision of reality as if it were their own. Encountering the sheer otherness of the caretaker shocks—and to the degree that there is "shock," there is also an eclipsing of the imaginative—even as a fundamental need for connection prompts us to adaptively comply.

"Making" a person see, as Rothko puts it, is different than inspiring a new way to imagine. That is why it is a rather commonplace experience to feel at least a modicum of disappointment watching the film version of a once-cherished book. The film's concretization of characters—portrayed by these particular actors, directed by this particular director, photographed at these particular angles —supersedes what one previously conjured imaginatively.

A far more malignant illustration of "making a person see" is the aesthetic sensibility of public art under totalitarian regimes. Whether in the form of monumental sculptures, grand architectural projects, or carefully orchestrated public ceremonies, art produced under totalitarian regimes is highly instrumental, aligned with the propagandistic aims of the state, and designed to project an image of strength, authority, and submission to an abstract unity. Art, although it may be technically innovative and skillful, can still be propaganda, telling people what they should think.

The totalitarian artistic impulse is often also remarkably concrete. There is no better example, perhaps, than Saddam Hussein's insistence that a cast of his own forearms be used as the mold for the Victory Arch in Baghdad commemorating the Iran–Iraq war. Theatrical concreteness—the arch, popularly known as the "hands of victory," displays a pair of outstretched arms holding crossed swords—has its allure. The fascination with such imagery, even if driven by a sense of horror or condemnation, also unwittingly contributes to totalitarianism's seductive power.[24]

Despite wide variations between fascist, totalitarian, and fundamentalist aesthetics, they all manage to pluck the chords of unconscious phantasy while suppressing the personally imaginative. What might begin as an imaginative vision—"things don't need to be the way they are"—hardens into a systematic concrete ideology—"things *must* be *only* this way"—brutally suppressing and extinguishing any further imaginative elaboration. Rather than a sometimes-fiery collection of arguments over competing claims—both within each individual and among members of society— an oppressive insistence on subservience to a singular vision takes hold. Since fascist, totalitarian, and fundamentalist states of mind are concerned primarily with eliminating uncertainty, compelling people to align with a totalistic claim on reality, and maintaining power over others, they cannot abide the inherently subversive, refractory, and irreconcilable contradictions of the personally imaginative.

The word silhouette derived from the name of a French finance minister, Étienne de Silhouette who, in the midst of a credit crisis in 1759, imposed economic austerity upon the French people. Silhouette's name became synonymous with anything made cheaply, as were the black-card cut-out profiles popular as inexpensive alternatives to the painted portrait miniatures prized by the elite. Silhouettes—made for the masses before the advent of mass production—were seen, in other words, as cheapened substitutes for more valued images. And so, too, can the imaginative serve many sensibilities: There is Coleridge's "higher worth" than that "allowed to the poor loveless ever-anxious crowd," and "Fancy," which recycles "fixities and definites," as well as totalistic visions that degrade and aim to extinguish the personally imaginative. Although liable to be debased and darkened, the imaginative irrepressibly seeks "forms for feelings," carrying at least the potential to resurface as nurse, guide, and guardian of one's heart.

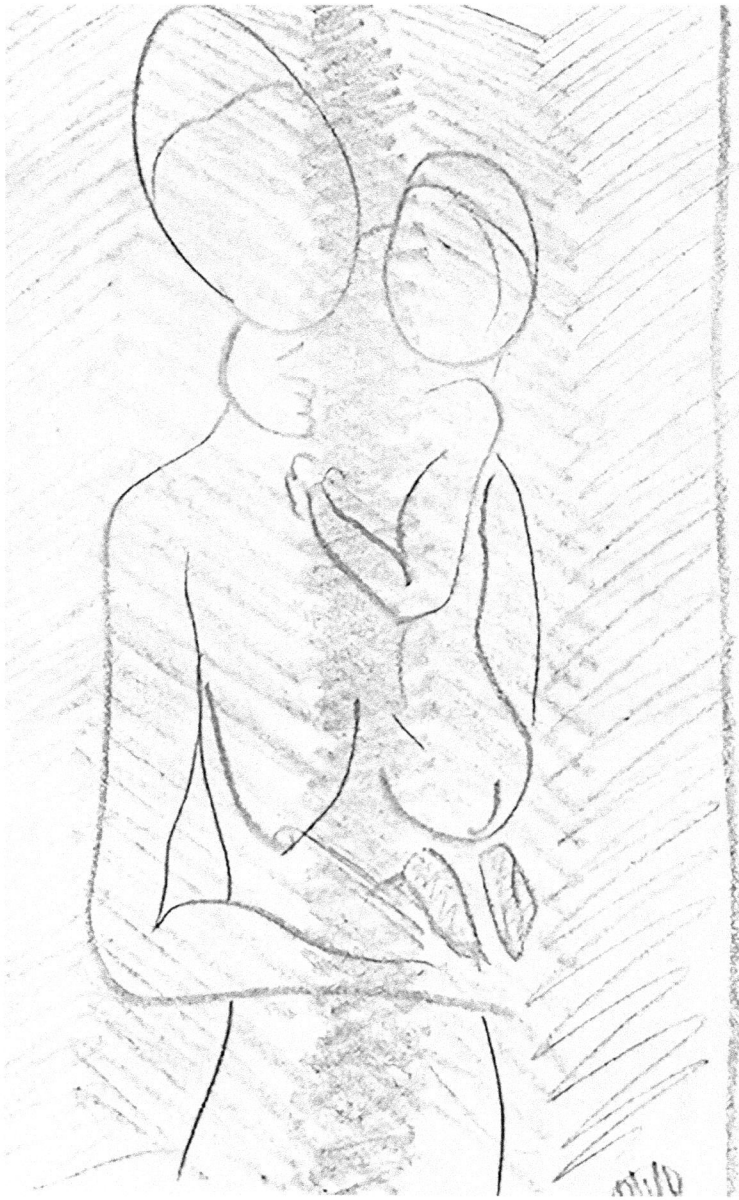

Chapter 4

Baby New to Earth and Sky

One of the biggest differences between psychoanalytic theorists, probably for reasons of temperament, is whether they are inclined to look primarily at babies' and mothers' separateness or at their embeddedness. For Klein, the vantage point is one of separateness. Baby's first gaze is that of an "I" looking at an object. Bodily sensations are interpreted as caused by an animated intentional other invested in either sustaining life or else hell bent on fragmenting and annihilating it. The infant is presumed to have an ego boundary that situates this other as either inside or outside and an active ability, in phantasy, to transport "not-me" entities across this boundary, into and out of itself.

But there are others—Michael and Enid Balint, Searles, Loewald, and Winnicott come to mind—for whom the first gaze mingles and blends a "yet-to-be I" and a "yet-to-be You." Michael Balint refers to this as a "harmonious interpenetrating mix-up."[1] The gaze of infant looking at mother looking at baby looking at mother meanders within an open field without discriminating analytically figure from ground. Seeing and being seen are one and the same. This syncretic perspective is eventually augmented by more focused and differentiated perception. But, from an unconscious point of view, embeddedness within a boundless whole remains a part of human experience—exhilarating and terrifying—perhaps most evident in the creative process of artists in every medium.[2]

From this not-yet-differentiated point of view, development does not proceed from one, to two, to three. We don't start out as a unified whole person, form a dyadic bond, and then, over time, traverse an oedipal dimension of tolerating a third. In the earliest stage of life, there is a psychic layer between mother and baby that is both an aspect of herself and of the baby. If all goes well in development (and that is a big "if"), baby gradually *emerges* (although never entirely) from this early intermingled state.

DOI: 10.4324/9781003536246-5

Freud generally tended to privilege the point of view of separateness. "Libido," which comes from the Latin meaning wish or desire, was posited as an energy that underlies the transformations of an inborn sexual instinct with regard to its object, aim, and source of excitation. Libido, in this sense, operates within a separate self. Yet, as is often the case with the vast expanse of Freud's oeuvre, one can also glean the opposite: Recognition of primary embeddedness. In Freud's version of the unconscious, there are no clear indices of an external reality from which the individual remains separate. In the last year of his life, Freud noted that we all *start out* believing ourselves to *be* the breast ("*Ich bin die Brust*/I am the breast"). Only later do we accept (although never entirely) that the breast is "not me" and so are forced to stake a claim to *have* it as our own.[3]

There is an implication here that Freud never fully elaborates: The creation of one's own world of meaning *precedes* socialization or input from external reality. Underlying the Freudian unconscious there is, to borrow Winnicott's language, an "incommunicado self,"[4] enclosed upon itself and enclosing within itself whatever is "presented" to it. It remains an open question, of course, whether this is truly the case, and, if so, how, when, and why the "social" weaves its way into the personal.

If one looks closely at the sketch at the start of the chapter—drawn by Winnicott—it is possible to detect elements of distinct separateness as well as areas in which the overlap between the figures makes it impossible to discern a boundary between them. The image captures a measure of both continuity with and emergence from embeddedness.

Much is involved in baby separating out "me" and "not-me," taking the leap of faith of putting psychological distance between self and object, bearing psychic pain when differences collide. Alfred Lord Tennyson gave poetic voice to this developmental process in a requiem for a beloved Cambridge friend:

> The baby new to earth and sky,
> What time his tender palm is rest
> Against the circle of the breast
> Has never thought that this is I;
>
> But as he grows he gathers much
> And learns the use of "I" and "me",

And finds "I am not what I see,
And other than the things I touch."

So rounds he to a separate mind
From whence pure memory may begin
As through the frame that binds him in
His isolation grows defined.[5]

Tennyson's requiem intuited a link between growth, grief, and a recognition of one's essential aloneness. As baby grows, he "gathers much." New horizons open as a not-me world is inferred, understood, and recognized as such. Baby gradually gathers himself up as well, cohering enough to face the world with agency and purpose. But "rounding to a separate mind" means also living with a measure of loss: Essential aloneness "grows defined." Going forward, baby must *imagine* his connectedness to others. Relationships may be our most vital form of illusion.

Emergence from embeddedness is not a solo voyage. "My idea is that the first imaginative perception can only arise out of a state of eager aliveness in two people," writes Enid Balint, "the infant with the potential for life and the mother alive inside herself and tuning in to the emerging infant."[6] An excited baby comes to mother's breast ready to conjure a sensual image of something fit to be attacked. When mother provides the actual breast, it corresponds in some way to their anticipation. They feel it to be the breast created in their own mind. The summoned or "hallucinated" breast is further enriched by the textured details—sights, feel, smell—of the actual one. In this way, baby "starts to build up a capacity to conjure up what is actually available."[7] It is not just that baby first creates the object and then (and only then) finds it. When finding an external object, they also create one in their mind. A foundation is laid down whereby we create in our minds what we find and we find what we create in our mind.

Given this delicate interplay, it is worth wondering: Where is the so-called "environment"? If the infant enters the world with a readiness and growing capacity to conjure what is actually available, is it not reasonable to presume that, at least to some extent, each baby creates their own personal environment? No two babies conjure what is actual in exactly the same way. Meanwhile, as baby is busy conjuring, there is also an actual external provision, which may or may not be good enough. No two mothers are "alive within herself" in exactly the same way. Nor is every baby alike in its capacity to make good-enough imaginative use of what is actual.

Environment is not a static "given" but an ever-shifting process of differentiation set in motion through repeated experiences of resonance and difference between a particular mother and baby. The "state of eager aliveness" between mother and baby is unpredictable. So, too, is how they structure each other reciprocally. In the unpredictability of the to-and-fro process, what we call "environment" is as much inside the individual as it is outside.

Looking to explain what moves a newborn to form a connection to the caretaking environment as it is being separated out, psychoanalytic theory placed great stock in the question: Is the infant "pleasure seeking" or "object seeking"? Whole schools of thought—one- and two-person psychologies—organized around this problem, although it might be a false one. There is another possible angle of vision: Perhaps baby's primary concern is neither pleasure nor objects but how the fabric of being is safeguarded as both individual and environment reciprocally structure each other.

One paradoxical function of imagining is to help discover and manage the contours of one's emerging separateness by generating an experience not exactly limited by our skin and not exactly the same as that which can be verified by our sense organs. The experience of emerging as a fragile but separate "I Am Me" is imaginatively elaborated so that we come alive in a new way. Concrete experiences—how tenderly or impatiently baby is held, whether spontaneous rhythms are allowed to run their natural course, how reliably needs, including the need to withdraw or down-regulate, are met—prompt psychic elaboration. These primal imaginings of actual experiences constitute baby's fabric of being. And no one can risk coming forth as an "I" that recognizes you as "you" unless, in the process of emergence, someone is there unobtrusively safeguarding that fabric of being.

Tennyson's baby, "new to earth and sky," encounters a gap between subject and object created through their growing separation ("I am not what I see/ And other than the things I touch"). Mother, too, must contend with this startling new situation. Whereas earlier, mother had felt baby to be a part of her physical self, she must now, in a sense, imaginatively *become* her baby through deep resonance with this piece of herself that is now "out there." Winnicott calls this state of mind "primary maternal preoccupation."[8] But "maternal preoccupation" is, perhaps, not the best choice of words.

"Go to the pine if you want to learn about the pine," wrote the 17th-century Japanese haiku poet Matsuo Bashō, "or to the bamboo if you want to learn about the bamboo. And in doing so, you must leave your subjective preoccupation with yourself." Bashō believed poetry was only possible if the poet "plunged deep enough" without "imposing … on the object." If the poet can do this, says Bashō, then "poetry issues of its own accord," and the poet will "see something hidden glimmering there."[9]

Winnicott's account is similar to what Bashō describes. Mother temporarily brackets her subjective preoccupation with herself and imaginatively "plunges" deep enough into baby's experience so as to know something about what baby needs. She cannot achieve this through effortful striving of a conscious will. It requires from her a measure of trust to allow something meaningful to emerge unbidden. By devotedly attending without imposing herself, "something glimmering there," as Bashō says, issues forth "of its own accord." Mother's capacity to do that is not based on some purported maternal instinct. It is a form of imaginative identification that draws upon a deep memory of being actually cared for by her own mother. What she "knows" is a form of knowledge transmitted through gestures across generations.

Both Bashō and Winnicott draw attention to a particular state of mind, which Iris Murdoch calls "an occasion for 'unselfing.'"[10] "Unselfing" is perhaps the greatest gift a caretaker can bestow. It lays down a foundation of basic trust, which allows a child to experience whatever is actually "out there" with curiosity and wonder rather than fear and agony. Throughout life, the imaginative use of curiosity and wonder will serve as reliable antidotes against sterility, disenchantment, despair, and alienation.

But here an objection is worth entertaining: Can mother really "put herself aside" and imaginatively become her baby? Can she "plunge deep enough," as Bashō advises, and actually "become one" with her baby? Bashō was an ascetic. The death of his mother shortly after a terrible house fire precipitated in him a desire to renounce the trappings of the material world and walk for many months with scant provisions, relying mainly on the kindness of Buddhist priests and fellow poets. Is the mother of a newborn expected to similarly sacrifice herself in some way? Does Freud's theory of renunciation reassert itself only in reverse, such that mother must be the one to renounce earlier pleasures so that her child can grow? Or, to state this more broadly: Do acts of imaginative empathy require relinquishing one's own first-person perspective?

The French psychoanalyst René Roussillon addresses these objections by suggesting a somewhat different metaphor. Mother and baby, he says, become potential "doubles." But doubles with a difference. Mother attunes emotionally to her infant, adapting her movements, gestures, and postures to those of her child in something like a "ballet." As mother shares her child's internal states, the infant "sees in the mother's face a reflection of this supportiveness as a double," which is "aesthetic, sensory and emotional."[11] Roussillon calls this a "narcissistic double." But Roussillon's "double" is not simply an identical copy of the original. If it were, it would be unable to reflect back a *personal* impression of what it sees. "The mother," writes Roussillon, "must therefore show that she is different, an other, through the way in which she reflects to her infant her sharing of emotions. The emotions and internal states … are similar, but not identical, to those of her infant."[12]

Roussillon's mother participates in the reciprocal structuring of self and other through repeated moments of resonance and difference, "unselfing," and personal expression of her distinctiveness. What matters is not merely *that* she reflects back but, as Roussillon says, "the *way* in which she reflects" back. How mother responds to dependency and assertion becomes inscribed in the infant's own experience of themselves as processes of a separate mind unfold naturally.

The "doubling" with a difference between mother and baby—sustaining a degree of distinctness while allowing baby to issue forth "on its own accord"—lays down what the Italian analyst Anna Ferutta calls "a legacy of experiences from which to start developing."[13] With this legacy, the newborn employs the leeway of their own imaginative capacities to make something of the actual world for themself.

The British analyst Kenneth Wright also addresses the imaginative bridging of the newly emerging gap between mother and newborn. Wright understands this gap not as the object loss psychoanalysis claims to be at the root of symbol formation but rather as a "looking space," within which "objects can be looked at but not touched"— that is, a space of consciousness itself.[14]

Wright places vision at the heart of baby's earliest adaptation to the separateness of their own mind, "the frame that binds him in," as Tennyson says. Many infancy researchers concur: Vision integrates messages received from all the other senses and introduces distal perception where, before, contact perception predominated. With distal perception, the child begins to apprehend continuity in time and coherence in space.[15] Eric Erickson suggests vision may be the "model of what is later felt to be the 'really real' enveloping the mere factual."[16]

Vision, of course, does not only refer to the capacity to see what is concretely before us here and now. It is also the power to foresee what may or may not come to be in the future, the liberty of mind to conjure images of possibilities, realistic and otherwise.

In Winnicott's sketch, prominent wavy lines emanate from and envelope mother and baby. This energy, or force field, also extends outward and beyond. How might we think about this? Winnicott seems to suggest a source of vitality and aliveness that has a root in a point of contact that is also one of separation.

Psychological aliveness cannot be taken for granted. While naturally given, it is at the same time contingent. Indeed, there is a precarious relationship between the environment and the psychosomatic equipment necessary to sustain aliveness.

Winnicott's image suggests that aliveness originates in an undifferentiated field which, only from an external point of view, appears as a newborn needing to be met by a responsive environment. Rather than a quality located within a distinct individual, aliveness has its roots in a psychic field between the two of them. Many of Winnicott's seminal formulations— spontaneous gesture, True Self, potential space, object use—are variations on the theme of how aliveness either grows and flourishes or is hidden or dampened as the developing child imaginatively elaborates a meaningful connection to the environment from which it is also differentiating itself. They are all ways of charting the gradual shift in the center of gravity of aliveness—which Winnicott also refers to as "being" so as to distinguish it from physical survival—from an undifferentiated field to the child's growing capacity to become an integrated unit able to sustain interplay between the imaginative and actual.

The notion of psychological aliveness enters psychoanalysis through the back door. It was only after Freud introduced his speculation about a death instinct that aliveness as distinct from either sexuality or self-preservation became something that needed to be accounted for. While the feasibility of a presumed death instinct generated much heat in psychoanalytic debate, it was actually Freud's introduction of the concept of Eros that was truly innovative. "The death instinct," writes Loewald "is really nothing new. ... What is new ... is the concept of Eros, the life or love instinct." It remained, Loewald argued, an "insoluble problem" for Freud to integrate Eros into his theory of instinct.[17] While, from a clinical point of view, the "death instinct" could at least be recognized as a biological version of the compulsion to repeat, when it came to Eros, Freud never quite figured out what to do with it.[18]

Indeed, one implication of Freud's way of thinking about the death instinct is that "aliveness" is merely a disruption of the inorganic that the death instinct strives to reconstitute. "The attributes of life," he notably remarked, were the result of "the action of a force of whose nature we can form no conception." He thought of it as a "tension" that arose somehow in previously inanimate matter, which, in the end, "strives towards its own dissolution."[19] Aliveness, for Freud, is a diversion on the way to death.

When looked at this way, Winnicott's oft-noted rejection of the death instinct is really less significant than his implicit celebration of a force constituting life. What Freud summarily dismissed as "the action of a force of whose nature we can form no conception" became, for Winnicott, an energy worthy of near reverence. "In each baby," he once remarked,

> is *a vital spark*, and this urge towards life and growth and development is a part of the baby, something the child is born with and which is carried forward in a way that we do not have to understand.[20]

The imaginative elaboration of aliveness, it could be said, is Winnicott's version of Eros. At the heart of Winnicott's work lies an abiding concern for the urge toward life and with the deadness that results from constrictions in the leeway for the psyche-soma to play with possibilities and imaginatively generate meaning. What makes people want to die or even take their own life is not inherent destructiveness but a traumatic loss of imaginative meaning-making.

It is worth returning to the beginning and introducing, or at least marking, an important caveat: Although psychoanalysts differ as to whether they are inclined to emphasize mother and baby's separateness and aloneness or their togetherness and relatedness, they nevertheless share western conceptions of individuality and of certain presumed boundaries to interdependence. But anthropological studies demonstrate enormous variation in how human communities imagine embeddedness and distinctiveness— both between individual people and even between humans and nonhumans. Philippe Descola's ethnographic studies of the Achuar people in

South America, for example, convincingly portray relationships between humans, forests, gardens, monkeys, snakes, and landscapes as alive and embedded in ways unimaginable to modern-day western observers.[21] For Westerners, the imaginative making of art, language, and culture is seen as essentially distinct from the natural world of plants, animals, geology, lightning, rainbows, and earthquakes. Humans may be affected by natural forces, but nature is understood to be separate and distinct from human intentionality. Not so for the Achuar, who operate without a fundamental divide between human and non-human, wild and domesticated, animate and inanimate, the individual and the collective. "When we try to pick out anything by itself," John Muir once wrote in his travel journal, "we find it hitched to everything else in the universe."[22] The Achuar lived always imagining this to be so.

Even within an increasingly "westernized" world, meaningful differences remain as far as the relative emphasis on independence or interdependence is concerned. Typical conversational patterns between mothers and infants in modern-day Japan and India, for example, are far more simultaneous, synchronous, and overlapping compared with the turn-taking and contingent responsiveness preferred in the U.S. and Europe. Clearly, the former assumes embedded togetherness, while the later privileges separateness.[23]

Many contemporary psychoanalysts explore inventive theories—field, attachment, interpersonal, relational, intersubjective—to describe and explain aspects of interdependence. Nevertheless, the primary area of concern of psychoanalysis remains congruent with its historic roots: Tennyson's "rounding to a separate mind, from whence ... isolation grows defined." Emergence from mother–child embeddedness is assumed to be an expectable and ultimately welcome feature of human development. And, as emergent separateness is negotiated, much hinges on both an individual's capacity for imaginative interplay with the actual environment and the actual environment's responsiveness to the individual's aliveness.

Once there is a nascent boundary between inner and outer, as tenuous and permeable as it might be, the question becomes: What *kind* of relationship will the emerging individual have with what is felt to be inside and perceived to be outside? Not only: What is the capacity to discern a landscape? But also: What makes the landscape shimmer? Psychic aliveness— whether thought of as Eros, life instincts, or a vital spark—implies an alive relationship between the imaginative and actual. Or, at least, that is one possible way to imagine how things might be.

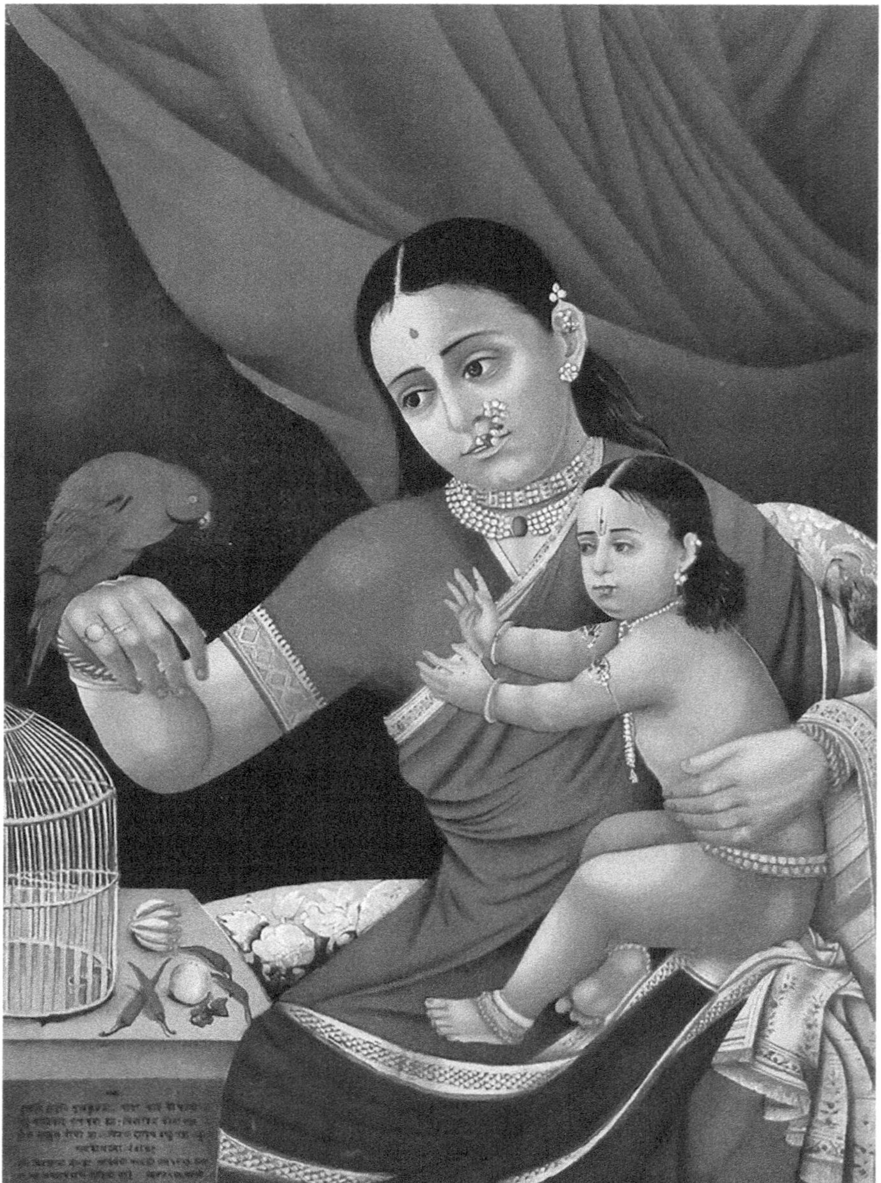

Chapter 5

Rama Playing

"Rama and His Mother With a Parrot" is an 1867 chromolithograph currently housed in the Wellcome Institute in London. Rama was the seventh, and one of the most popular, avatars of the Hindu god Vishnu. The epic tale of his life and travails, the Ramayana, is a narrative allegory at the core of Hindu religious belief. Rama's mother, Kausalya, was the senior queen-consort of one of ancient India's northern realms. Perched on her wrist is a parrot, a creature revered in Indian art as messenger, storyteller, and teacher as well as symbol of love and passion. According to Adrain Plau, an expert in early Hindi and South Asian manuscripts, "the parrot might suggest the divine reality underpinning things as they appear, which is a recurring theme of the 'god-as-child' motif."[1] The parrot sparks Rama's interest, and he reaches out with desire.

The image shimmers with the rich abundance of courtly material culture as well as the powerful symbolic significance imbuing deity, queen, and sacred creature. What happens, however, if, rather than seeing these figures as mythic beings, we allow ourselves to imagine them as mere flesh and blood—mother, child, and enticing object—engaged in an ordinary family drama?

Kausalya provides the setting for Rama to be excitedly curious about an object felt to be part of her. Curiosity signals imaginative stirrings. Rama desires contact with his mother's surround because he believes in the possibility of wanting and connecting without persecutory pain. Kausalya herself is a pleasure- and object-seeker—holding, handling, and presenting the world in small doses to her child; seeing the world from both her own and Rama's point of view; taking delight in Rama's delight; and allowing him to gradually discover a world not of his own making.

DOI: 10.4324/9781003536246-6

But, and this is crucial, Rama is no mere passive recipient of Kausalya's ministrations. He brings an idiosyncratic spark, an imaginative vitality that works in alliance with the world's offerings. It is not only that Kausalya's attunement enables Rama to thrive; Rama's imaginative aliveness helps his mother remain good enough! Rama may be excitedly aroused by the object of his desire but he also tracks what mother communicates about his excitement. Does she feel it is safe? Will she enjoy his taking hold of the parrot or fear the damage he may do? Must Rama break free of her to have what he wants?

Kausalya and Rama do not only share an object of joint attention. As Rama's inventiveness overlaps with Kausalya's attentiveness, there is a vibrant, though fragile, "moment of meeting"—Daniel Stern calls this a "shared feeling voyage"[2]—a reciprocal recognition wherein "I sense that you sense that I sense ..."[3] Mother and child are *living an experience together*.[4] In this moment, how Rama knows himself has an area of overlap with the way he is known by another.[5] Living experiences together does not mean each person experiences exactly the same thing. But they do help a child accrue confidence in their own vitality. They make the landscape shimmer. And they instill a desire to employ imaginative capacities not only defensively to avoid reality but to create and recreate the moment of meeting and discovery of that "something more" than what concrete reality alone has to offer.[6]

Rama and Kausalya are also playing together. Playing, which in its Old English connotation meant to take a risk, to expose oneself to danger from someone or something, is not about fun, amusement, lightheartedness, or having a good time. From a psychoanalytic point of view, child's play is serious business. Playing has sometimes been understood as an attempt to master past feelings of traumatic helplessness. By symbolically repeating experiences not yet mastered in reality, the playing child turns passive suffering into active mastery. Playing has also been seen as something necessary in the present to cathartically release pent-up emotions or surplus energy through kinetic activity. But psychoanalysis also leaves room for a future orientation in its functional understanding of playing as an opportunity to acquire and exercise emerging faculties. Through playing, children prepare themselves to live in the adult world they must eventually inhabit.

One need not choose among these theories. No matter how play's "purpose" is understood—whether oriented to past, present, or future—Plato's early formulation remains relevant: The root of true play, Plato claimed, is the "habitual tendency of every living creature to leap."[7] Using ground as a springboard, animals test the leeway of limits. In so doing, they aim to defy gravity while landing safely and securely.

In humans, the leap entails a *particular state of mind*. While playing, we enter a primary area of experiencing that precedes any differentiation between psychic and external reality. It is worth pausing on this matter: While, from an external point of view, it may seem that playing is a projection of subjective reality onto the external world—a child's wish to move at great speed or be powerful is gratified by racing a toy car across a floor—this obscures the actual experience of playing. Winnicott's contention that playing is exciting because "it deals with the existence of a precarious borderline between the subjective and that which can be objectively perceived"[8] does not mean a mixing, an overlapping, or some combination of psychic contents and external reality but a state of mind in its own right.

Playing is a form of illusion, an area of experiencing that *precedes* any distinction between fact and phantasy. In Winnicott's language, it is an opportunity "to experience separation without separation."[9] The experience is one in which the binary structure—inner/outer—does not yet figure. That is why playing (and cultural life in general) "cannot be placed in the inner or personal psychical reality, because it is not a dream" but neither can it be "said to be part of external relationships because it is dominated by dream."[10] This "no-man's land between the subjective and the objectively perceived"[11] belongs to neither because the distinction between these realms is not part of the experience.

The root of playing resides in an infant's creative impulse or gesture. The baby has a nascent need, which seeks fulfillment. If the need intensifies, the baby attempts to create the need-fulfilling situation by hallucinating. In and of themselves, creative gestures are little more than impotent hallucinations; they cannot actually fulfill the need. But they do carry the potential to be realized if met by a caretaker. "We have to say," writes Winnicott, "that the baby created the breast, but could not have done so had not the mother come along with the breast just at that moment."[12] Note Winnicott's language: The mere conjuring of the breast is not what is creative. It is the experience of having the conjuring actualized by someone not yet perceived as external.

The illusion created out of need has, from the infant's point of view, "real existence," before and without awareness of external reality.[13]

While illusions may be situated *between* hallucinations and delusions, they are an area of experiencing in their own right.[14] Hallucinations are purely subjective "dream phenomena that have come forward into the waking life."[15] Delusions, a "hallmark of madness,"[16] occur when a person claims something as objective reality when it is not. Illusions are not an overlapping of hallucinations (something merely subjective) and delusions (insistence that external reality is something it is not).

The earliest experiences of illusion are but the first step in a developing series: Creating the breast, transitional phenomenon, playing, and cultural life. Each step in the series is simultaneously self-generated and actual without any need to maintain a distinction between the two. They are a "resting place out of which a creative reaching out can take place,"[17] precisely because the individual is temporarily relieved of the strain of keeping inner and outer separate but interrelated. In a certain sense, it is playing, not necessity, which is the real mother of invention.

Playing is a psychic leap—perhaps a leap of faith—back to an originary state of mind in which the question "Is it real or not real?" has no meaning. To pose that question is to destroy the experience. While playing, we are not living in two worlds simultaneously. We are in the midst of a *singular uncontested experience*. Put differently: From an external vantage point, playing entails a state of being in which the actual world is accepted for what it is while simultaneously elaborated, rearranged, and challenged in accordance with one's imaginative sensibility. But the felt experience is not one of making something out of a pre-existing world. It is the creation of a world of one's own that exists without undue dissonance, even though an outside observer might think of it as "not real."

Playing is possible only if one can allow imaginative use of the world's affordances, intuit possibilities for potential, and bear subjective realities that might otherwise persecute from within. Playing entails excitedly reaching out to the unknown and disposing of things when you've gotten from them what you want. It is common for children to become overstimulated or frightened by their own imaginings. No one can truly play if too fearful. When afraid, there may be frenzied discharge of tension or distraction from upset, but activity of this sort is not playing.

As any parent knows, playing is precarious. Someone can easily get hurt. If pulled too quickly back into what is actual or subjugated to the "not-me" experience of external time, children collapse into rageful despair ("Time for dinner!"). Many "tantrums" are impotent protests over too sudden a loss of the potential space of playing. Children's games, with all their space–time delineations—ball parks, game boards, time limits, strict procedural rules, turn taking—were probably invented to contain the threatening intensity of excitements aroused in playing, excitements that can easily overwhelm the individual, whether child or adult. Games, it has been said, are "a form of war which can occur only amongst those who are at peace"[18]

Imaginative playing is at times solitary, an instance of being alone in the presence of another, and at times participatory and interactive, enriched by mutual adaptation and reciprocal exchange with a good-enough playmate. While mother might "spark" or evoke baby's playfulness, it is bothersome for her to try to extract it, interrupt it, or insist baby remain engaged with the object of his desirous curiosity once he is done with it.

Playing, in other words, is both a state of mind and also an experiment in sociability, sustainable only under certain conditions: How much leeway can be granted before it interferes with the leeway of another? Within relationships, it is an alternative to sadomasochism, cannot be scripted, has no predetermined end, and does not traffic in domination and submission. Imaginative playing engenders the erotic but ceases in states of coercion, contraction, or withdrawal. Certainly, what we call "sexuality" has little meaning without erotic imagining.

Picture this: A little boy in the shallow part of a public swimming pool. He hasn't yet learned to swim very well. Were you to ask him, however, he would insist otherwise. His confidence far exceeds his competence. One might say this is a triumph of the imaginative over the actual.

The little boy dons shark goggles, a rubber fin protruding atop his head. He is excited to feel ferocious. Lurking about, boy-shark soon spots his prey: A girl splashing about innocently nearby. Stealthily approaching from the side, he simulates hissing shark sounds. The little girl, caught off guard, is momentarily startled. But, once she makes sense of her predicament, she bops the little boy on his fin. "Just because you have a shark mask," she admonishes him, "doesn't mean you are *really* a shark!" Standing tall, the boy-shark realizes, probably for the first time, that the girl is much bigger than he is. Slinking away to safer water, he displays his teeth, growls, and barks emphatically for her to hear, "I AM a shark!"

From the point of view of the little girl, he is *nothing but* a little boy masquerading as a shark. But, from his point of view, he both *is* and *is not* a shark. He is engaged in a type of play for which we employ the word "pretend." As a child pretends, he is not only projecting phantasy but nurturing and practicing a vital skill: Exploring the leeways and limits of imaginative life, distinguishing the delusional from the illusional. It is an enormous developmental achievement to smoothly express in behavior an imagistic pattern—I am a shark hunting prey—while not confusing it with literal reality.[19] As Vygotsky puts it, "in play the child is always above his average age, above his daily behavior … it is as though he were a head taller than himself."[20]

Pretending affords the possibility of *unbelieving* internal phantasies through exploration of the playful possibilities of "make-believe" based on pretense. Current developmental research illuminates how self-reflexivity coincides with the emergence of pretend play. Only gradually does a child grasp that representations can be freed from their referents; that appearances and reality are not equivalent; that there are subtleties of secrecy and lying.[21] Before that, children operate in what Fonagy[22] refers to as a mode of psychic equivalence, behaving as though thoughts faithfully mirror the actual world. But pretend play facilitates a more solid appreciation that things may not be what they appear to be, that another person may perceive external reality differently, and that a person can hold different beliefs at different times. Healthy children absorbed in pretend play can know these things and nevertheless allow themselves to temporarily enter a state of mind in which none of that matters. Imaginatively reaching for what is beyond their literal grasp, the child as author, director, and actor uses things in the real world to exercise the leeway of psyche-soma over the possibilities of things while learning to recognize limits. Make-believe is a way of making beliefs about what is actual.

But pretending needs protecting. Consider this illustration from *Homo Ludens*, Johan Huizinga's historical study of play:

A father found his four year old son sitting at the front of a row of chairs, playing "trains." When he kissed his son the boy said: "Don't kiss the engine Daddy, or the carriages won't think it's real."[23]

So long as a child holds onto the uncontested state of mind, they are able to play. If reality is introduced too abruptly, reminding them that they are "just playing," the child will be dislocated from pretend mode. Should the imagistic story become so "real" as to be experienced as actual, the child may panic about having lost any way out or back. Either way, genuine vitality evaporates. It is challenging to remain imaginatively alive as brakes are placed on the imaginative; to both imagine *and* encounter things as they truly are without needing to attend to which is which.

The foreclosure of the state of mind necessary for playing is a far cry from what is commonly thought of as "giving up childish illusions." Nearly the opposite: It signals the individual has likely experienced some degree of premature or, worse, catastrophic disillusionment. The damaging or even violent obtrusion of a person's natural discovery and creation of the world in accordance with their readiness profoundly affects well-being, impeding growth of individuals as well as societies. Playing may be precarious, but its absence is deadly serious.

Chapter 6

What Do We Talk About When We Talk About Aggression?

Pitseolak Niviaqsi was an Inuit master carver and printmaker from Kinngait (Cape Dorset), a hamlet on one of Canada's Arctic islands. He was renowned for statues and lithographs of Sedna, the Inuit mythological "Mother of the Sea," as well as sensitive portrayals of actual mothers and their children. His art moves seamlessly between these registers.

In this polished serpentine sculpture, Niviaqsi captures mother battling both nature's elements and the elemental nature of her child. As a life-long resident of the frigid Hudson Straits, he no doubt witnessed Inuit mothers battling headwinds as their headstrong toddlers rode roughshod over them. From one angle, mother's persistence and fortitude are palpable. From another, the emotion shifts. Mother's internal struggle becomes more apparent as the child pulls relentlessly at her braid.[1] Niviaqsi offers an intimate and personal glimpse of resolve and restraint; mother survives by simultaneously resisting and yielding to her child.

The child has aggressively and excitedly gotten hold of a piece of mother's body. He wants very badly to do something with it, even though he may not know what it is he wants to do: Cling for dear life or free himself of her clutches? Burrow into her or pull her into himself? Whatever he's imagining, he is making sense of the thrills and terrors of his burgeoning autonomy. He no doubt feels mother's opposition, her efforts to quash his freedom of movement. So he's also learning to contend with the impact of her disapproval, the problem of another person's desire. He may have intense, even harrowing, feelings about all this. What memory traces remain from such moments? Might these eventually be elaborated into a phantasy of renewal through violence?

And what about mother? While she might be reassured by baby's rambunctious aliveness, she's alert to a potentially alarming crescendo. Focused

DOI: 10.4324/9781003536246-7

on moving forward, she nevertheless closely tracks the clutching child on her backside. Is he feeling thrill or terror? The tug at her braid hurts. It would be natural to want to rid herself of the merciless creature evincing no qualms about the pain he inflicts. But she's devoted; there's work to be done and a child to protect.

It is also worth wondering how this hearty child registers mother's struggle, the assault upon her sense of adequacy as a mother. It is likely the child absorbs, if only enigmatically, something of mother's struggle, her experience of falling short, the repeated loss of her center of gravity followed by either her devoted desire to set things right or collapse into dispirited despair or retaliation. A mother who can regain her equilibrium and effectively resist and yield to such relentless demands helps the child discover a robust sense of an external other that can joyfully be used rather than sadistically abused.

Clashes between mother and child began long before the image captured in Niviaqsi's sculpture. From the moment a fetus is lodged in mother's body, the two are engaged in battle—over resources, nutrients, territory— suggestive of "Either you or me!" or "We both must live or die together!" How does mother feel about this potentially mortal conflict where life is literally at stake? What can we say about baby's early aggression?

It is easy to forget that, while Freud emphasized that "men are not gentle creatures; they are, on the contrary, creatures among whose instinctual endowments is to be reckoned a powerful share of aggressiveness,"[2] he nevertheless was circumspect about positing a *separate* aggressive instinct. In part, this was rooted in his reluctance to attribute to a single instinct something that was an essential feature of every instinct—a press for activity to achieve an aim, even if the aim be a passive one. Over time, Freud's emphasis on aggression broadened considerably. Yet, even late in life, speculating about a purported death instinct, he explodes traditional understandings of aggression as a force aiming to inflict harm upon others. Instead, Freud's death instinct manifests as aggression toward the *self*, a drive within an organism to return to an inorganic state, and the breaking up of unities created through Eros. This is a far cry from what is commonly thought of as "hostility" or "aggression."

Nevertheless, psychoanalysis has elucidated many so-called aggressive phantasies—cannibalistic devouring, violent expulsions, perverse punishments, sadomasochistic entanglements. How these phantasies are experienced and the extent to which they may or may not be actualized, either symbolically or literally, are traditionally believed to depend on aggression's fusion with and de-fusion from sexuality. Or on the interplay between life and death instincts or loving and hateful feelings.

At the same time, perhaps no issue divides psychoanalysts as does the question how best to understand aggression in human experience: Is it simply reactive to frustration? A self-protective response to perceived threat? Or are hate and sadism inherently destructive impulses threatening to damage others and potentially savage one's own mind from within? And at what point can we say that a child "means" or "intends" the harm they inflict? To borrow from Raymond Carver: What do we talk about when we talk about "aggression"?

However one is inclined to view these matters, it is worth wondering what bearing aggression may have on imaginative life. And vice versa. Or, perhaps a better way of putting it: How intimately are the imaginative and aggressive intertwined?

While the Hebrew Bible may seem an odd source to consider when thinking about the interplay of the imaginative and the aggressive, there is good reason to do so. For it is precisely in the opening chapters of the Book of Genesis that western civilization first articulates the idea that imagining coincides with aggressive transgression. From its inception, imagining is intimately bound with an aggressive act.

Considering ancient texts such as the Hebrew Bible carries an obvious risk: Can contemporary consciousness reappropriate the meanings or comprehend the lived experience of such an earlier time? Isn't it a fool's errand to try to retrieve some original intention from an ancient text? These problems are actual. Nevertheless, there is benefit in allowing the old and new to meet up and see what emerges when their horizons converge. The intertwining of the aggressive and imaginative can be seen to have a genealogy all its own.

The ancient Biblical term for the imaginative is the word "*yetzer*," which derives from the same root (יצר/YZR) as the words "creation," "creator," and "create." The most recent modern English translation of the Bible uses the phrase "every scheme of his heart's devising" for the Hebraic yetzer.[3] Yetzer was understood in the Biblical context as the human creative drive to imitate God's own creation. When the serpent entices humans with the "knowledge of good and evil," he specifically promises Adam and Eve they will be "like gods," with the capacity to create a world of their *own* making. They, too, will have a passion for the possible. But, to obtain godlike power,

Adam and Eve must aggress against God's law and eat forbidden fruit. This exact theme is reprised centuries later in the myth of Prometheus transgressing against Zeus by bestowing fire upon humankind. Both Adam's yetzer and Prometheus's fire express the power of the imaginative to shape, form, and figure as gods do. This appropriation or imitation of God's capacity to create is both an act of liberation and a curse, forever carrying the stigma of aggressive transgression. The freedom to imagine threatens the power status quo.

Erich Fromm is the rare psychoanalyst who noted the allusive interplay between the imaginative and transgressive, linking it to notions of good and evil. "With reference to the mind, the term 'yetzer,' means imaginings (good or evil)," writes Fromm. In fact, the "problem of good and evil arises only when there is imagination." Furthermore, people "can become more evil and more good … precisely because of that specifically human quality—imagination."[4]

Consistent with his Orthodox Jewish upbringing, Fromm highlights the ethical consciousness of good and evil, a point of view Freud had little interest in. As Freud wrote to his friend Oskar Pfister, "ethics are remote from me. I do not break my head very much about good and evil."[5] Nevertheless, Freud did not shy away from describing "evil inclinations"—the biblical "yetzer"—particularly in the context of resistance to his treatment.[6]

Biblical accounts of yetzer, however, do not only suggest *ethical* consciousness. They are also coincident with the emergence of *temporal* consciousness. As the imaginative projects a human future, the individual is prone to pride, presumption, failures, and grandiosity. And, as a temporal past comes into consciousness, the individual weighs memory of what occurred against what they imagine might have occurred otherwise. As a result, new experiences of loss, shame, regret, guilt, and remorse come to the fore.

One of Melanie Klein's contributions was to suggest there is no such thing as an instinct without an object. What the Biblical account adds is the idea that there is no such thing as an impulse without imaginings. It is not a coincidence that, in modern Hebrew usage, the word yetzer has assumed the meaning "impulse" or "inclination." These imaginings—images inciting the heart's desires—shouldn't be reduced to or be conflated with unconscious phantasies. There may be, for example, a fixed phantasy of restoring a lost Eden coexistent with nascent imaginings of moving from the security of what is known toward that which is not. Imaginings allow for a degree of freedom to transcend what exists in the direction of what might actually come to be. *Yetzer* is the play of possibilities.

While the Biblical account of yetzer may shed light on western civilization's early *conceptual* intertwining of the aggressive and the imaginative, it tells us little about the *developmental* interplay. For that, one needs to consider the *physical* aspect of aggression, so well captured in Niviaqsi's image of the Inuit child and mother.

Freud famously took as a starting point the presumption that the "I" is "first and foremost a bodily 'I,'"[7] which is "ultimately derived from bodily *sensations*, chiefly from those springing from the surface of the body."[8] In a variety of ways, Freud wrestled with what is distinctive about aggressivity in terms of the body. And although, as mentioned, he refrained from positing a separate aggressive instinct, there were points at which he played with the possibility of a so-called "instinct to master" based on the "somatic muscu-lature." He suggested this non-sexual instinct, which aimed to seize, sub-jugate, or dominate, was the force behind the primal cruelty of children.[9]

What Freud never fully resolved, nor has psychoanalysis since, is whether this "primal cruelty" necessarily involves an actual *intention* to harm. Freud's earliest iteration of an instinct to master places it before the emer-gence of pity or sadism. As such, its original aim is not to inflict suffering; it simply fails to take into account the existence of the other person. After introducing the idea of the death instinct, however, Freud came around to the idea that sadistic cruelty is a diversion outward of the destructive force originally aimed at the "I" itself. But, even in this rendering, the extent to which the primal impetus of aggression is to actually hurt another or a matter of self-preservation remains ambiguous.

The ambiguities in Freud's account reappear as disagreements among his followers. And no one elaborated the imagined dramas associated with the purported death instinct as thoroughly as Klein did. She saw the infant's world as an animate personalized one in which distressing sensations of hunger and thirst stimulate phantasies of objects assaulting from within. While not a biologist, Klein was trying to think through how the biologic-ally endowed fear of dying was imagined as the concrete presence of an evil force intent upon annihilation. "Seething with murder in his heart,"[10] baby employs the only defenses at their disposal: Hateful attacks on their persecutors and phantasies of transporting the bad objects out of themself.

The infant then anticipates retaliation. The evil presence will surely return hate as murderous as their own.

This mutually assured persecution continues until "reality" eventually dawns on the newborn. Baby comes to realize their imaginings are misguided, the enemy has been misidentified so to speak. The evil presence is one and the same "person" as the life-sustaining object that nourishes. Baby becomes anxious in a new way as they grasp they are attacking not only all that is bad but also all that is good. One way the child copes with this anxious guilt is by imagining ways to repair the damage they have done.

In a certain sense, the Biblical "*yetzer*"—the imagined desires of the heart—resurfaces in Klein's theory. Her use of the word "phantasy" to describe baby's mind can hardly be understood as "unconscious" in any strict sense of the term. Instead, it seems consistent with both the German "*Phantasie*," a word connoting the creative activity animating the imaginative world, and with Aristotle's "*Phantasia*," the activity of the mind mediating between sensation and reason. In the same way that yetzer creates a world of its own making, Klein's phantasies are baby's way of creating order out of chaos. They are imaginings of good and evil that provide a meaningful interpretation of physical experience.

It is highly unlikely Winnicott was familiar with the Hebraic *yetzer*. Nevertheless, he intuited an additional way Klein's view of early aggression mirrored the Biblical account, only this time with a Christian twist. In his forceful rejection of the death instinct, Winnicott noted that it was, in essence, "a reassertion of the principle of *original sin*."[11] One can certainly find among Jewish commentators the idea that "*yetzer*" (and the "evil inclination"—"*yetzer hara*"—in particular) is, as the medieval Spanish philosopher ibn Pekuda puts it, "interwoven in the forces of your soul and intertwined in the order of your spirit."[12]

But, generally speaking, the Hebraic understanding of yetzer is that humans are prone to *misusing the natural survival needs* of the physical body. So, for example, the need for food can, through the imaginings of the yetzer, morph into gluttony; the desire to procreate can go astray and become sexual promiscuity; the need for rest can degenerate into sloth. In a certain sense, what is called an "evil inclination" arises when one imagines one needs more than one actually does. The death instinct, however, like the Christian doctrine of Original Sin, suggests something far more radical: Humans are born with a tainted nature from which there is no escape. For Christians, the taint is one of concupiscence, a proclivity to sin, which Augustine called "hurtful desire" condemning humanity to perdition.[13] For Klein, the taint is an inherent destructiveness ever threatening to fragment and annihilate the world and oneself.

Winnicott not only objected to the reassertion of original sin into psychoanalytic thinking but points to alternative ways of thinking about the roots of aggression. To be clear: There are elements of Klein's narrative Winnicott readily accepted. He had no trouble acknowledging, for example, the reality of talion dread, the splitting of the object into good and bad, or that hate, sadism, and even strivings to subjugate and prevail over others—whether self-protective or self-aggrandizing—are all quite real. As a practicing child psychiatrist, he was familiar with both affectively evoked aggression in response to perceived threats and predatory aggression directed toward the destruction of prey. He recognized *disordered* expressions of aggression in the form of reactions toward disappointing, neglectful, or dangerous caretakers, *deficits* in affectionate relations or self-reflective function, and *deviance*, whereby violence can become habitual, thrilling, or addictive.[14] But, for Winnicott, *all these come later* in development. They are not the lived experience of *infants*. So long as there is a devoted caretaker holding the situation in time, primal imaginings of an evil mother aren't inevitable. Recognizing distortions in the use of aggression potential is not the same as claiming an inherent taint in the human condition.

Winnicott's understanding of both the origins and nature of aggression never settled, which is why he sometimes appears to contradict himself. For example, at times he speaks of "aggression" as "almost synonymous with activity," even prenatally.[15] In other places, he reserves the term to describe a more specific impulse that occurs later in development with greater integration of the personality. As Winnicott arrives at new formulations, he doesn't acknowledge abandoning older ones. He simply keeps reworking the problem. Still, Winnicott's sensibility inclined him toward a view of aggression distinct from the ones put forth by Freud and Klein.

As a pediatrician, Winnicott was intrigued by the ebb and flow between disarray and coherence punctuating the experience of a newborn. How did all the wriggling, twitching, squirming, and flailing, not to mention the rhythmic throbbing of heart and lungs, innervations, fluctuations in pressure and temperature, and seemingly random kinetic arousals, gradually all come together into a more or less organized entity with a personal sense of aliveness? And what conditions *external* to the infant's body help establish and ensure baby's sense of "going-on-being" and "continuity of existence"?[16]

Only through his personal analysis was Winnicott first able to overcome his medical training and see babies as something more than the sum of their body parts—that is, as full human beings. He confessed remaining "extremely sympathetic with ... anybody who can't see babies as human, because I absolutely couldn't, however I used to try."[17] And so he remained captivated by when and how the array of the psyche-soma's imaginative elaborations add up and cohere into a whole person, felt and recognized as such.

Like Freud, Winnicott presumes the "I" starts out as a bodily "I." But, unlike Freud, he doesn't focus on the ego as a perceptual apparatus derived from sensations arising from the body surface. Instead, Winnicott emphasizes the building up of an "I" through imaginative elaboration of physical aliveness. And it is with the imaginative elaboration of early motility in particular that Winnicott most clearly identifies the intertwining of an aggressive "I" and the imaginative.

Beginning *prenatally*, motility, kinetic arousals, "the sudden movement of limbs that make the mother say she is feeling a quickening"[18]—are all an inherent part of aliveness. To get to the root of aggression, says Winnicott, it is necessary to look at this "fact of infantile movement"[19] and to "go back to the impulses of the foetus, that which makes for movement rather than stillness, to the aliveness of tissues and to the first evidence of muscular eroticism."[20] The aggression implicit in the aliveness and motility of the developing fetus and newborn is, he says on more than one occasion, "part of the primitive expression of love."[21]

There are many implications in Winnicott's seemingly straightforward description, some of which are startling from a psychoanalytic point of view. First, Winnicott stands Freud's radical antithesis between life and death instincts on its head. Rather than a fundamental antagonism, he is suggesting a shared root in a single vital "life force." What interests Winnicott is the "conversion of this life force into aggression potential."[22]

In addition, Winnicott sees the "erotism" engendered in the muscles and movements as distinct from what psychoanalysis identifies as "instinctual" or drive-based. It does not follow the pattern of "rising tension of general and local excitement, climax and detumescence ... followed by a period of lack of desire."[23] Instead, the experience involved in the movement of muscles and other tissues is of a different order than the instinctual erotism associated with erotogenic zones.[24]

Third, as Winnicott "dissects down"[25] to what he believes lies beneath or before "jealousy, envy, anger at frustration, the operation of the instincts that we name sadistic,"[26] he reaches the conclusion that natural bodily aggression precedes aggression against the object. That these early life gestures inflict harm on mother does not mean they carry hateful or sadistic *intent*. Because a baby kicks in the womb does not mean they are trying to kick their way out. Similarly, a newborn thrashing away with their arms or vigorously chewing the nipple is not meaning to hit or hurt. People do not start out loving and hating. They start out alive in the world and to the world.

Finally, whereas Freud presumed that early self-directed movements are simply one of the various *functions* of the ego, Winnicott sees them as *constitutive* of the self.[27] Motility establishes and gives organized existence to an organism otherwise in disarray. Winnicott even wildly speculates that the quality of fetal motility determines the actual experience of birth itself. Because a fetus is capable of swimming movements and reptation, a mode of propulsion forward without the use of limbs, normal births afford an opportunity for the fetus to exert a degree of self-agency. Given more or less accurate timing—Winnicott often introduces an element of luck into his accounts—the fetus need not necessarily experience traumatic helplessness traversing the birth canal. Rather than a sense of "being in the grips of something external," the actual birth "can easily be felt by the infant ... to be a successful outcome of personal effort."[28]

After birth, self-directed movements and collisions help facilitate the emergence of a psychological self from the rich amalgam of sensations enveloping the newborn. Friction-inducing, collision-prone gestures do not arise merely as a reaction to frustration of desire. Babies take pleasure in experiencing obstacles and opposition and are enriched by bumping up against a not-me world. The pleasure discovered in opposition is not one of hatred or hostility. It precedes them. Winnicott goes so far as to claim that, since the motility impulse cannot "give any satisfactory experience *unless* there is opposition,"[29] babies actively *seek* opportunities to experience obstacles. In fact, the baby's motility impulse "needs to find opposition ... it needs something to push up against."[30] The discovery of opposition met through movement helps shape the contours of what is inside and what is out, the "early recognition of a Not-Me world, and an early establishment of the Me."[31] Eventually, the healthy individual "can enjoy going around looking for appropriate opposition."[32] Here, then, is a radical implication: The impulse to move *becomes* aggressive when it meets opposition. And because of the aggression that develops out of the impulse, the infant needs an *external* object and not only a *satisfying* object. There is a striving to place things outside of omnipotent control, an urge toward growth, a desire to find something external, and therefore painfully real, to love.

For Winnicott, the *physical* aliveness of the infant is intimately intertwined with *psychic* aliveness. In the beginning, they are so intertwined that "the psyche and the soma are not to be distinguished except according to the direction from which one is looking."[33] What psychic aliveness means is the imaginative elaboration of the physical arousals and gestures. The soma is awash in movements, and the psyche is animated. What we call "experience" is both physical and non-physical. "Ideas," Winnicott notes, "accompany and enrich bodily function, and bodily functioning accompanies and realizes ideation."[34] These "ideas"—or images constituting the building blocks of "thought"—arise spontaneously.

In a certain sense, physical motility becomes the template for psychic motility. Both describe movements that are non-defensive, uninhibited, and flow from "the centre" or "core" of the individual.[35] They convey how a person moves in the world. To the extent that imaginative ideas about the meanings and intentions related to physical encounters build up spontaneously, external reality is experienced as something personal and meaningful. If there is, instead, a pattern of environmental impingement upon, or retaliation against, the free flow of movement—whether physical or psychic—the aggression potential becomes dissociated or inhibited. External reality is then felt primarily as an imposition from beyond, and the individual fails to evolve.[36]

It is worth returning to Niviaqsi's statue. The Inuit mother, certainly in her present circumstances, cannot simply yield to her toddler's wild ride. A part of her may want to lash out. She may also recall him flailing about as an infant, distraught by forces roiling within, and how calm he grew when swaddled. She tracks the rising crescendo of his exuberance, intuiting the tipping point at which it may become more menacing, to her or even to himself. One can imagine her a good-enough mother who allows leeway but won't let anyone get hurt.

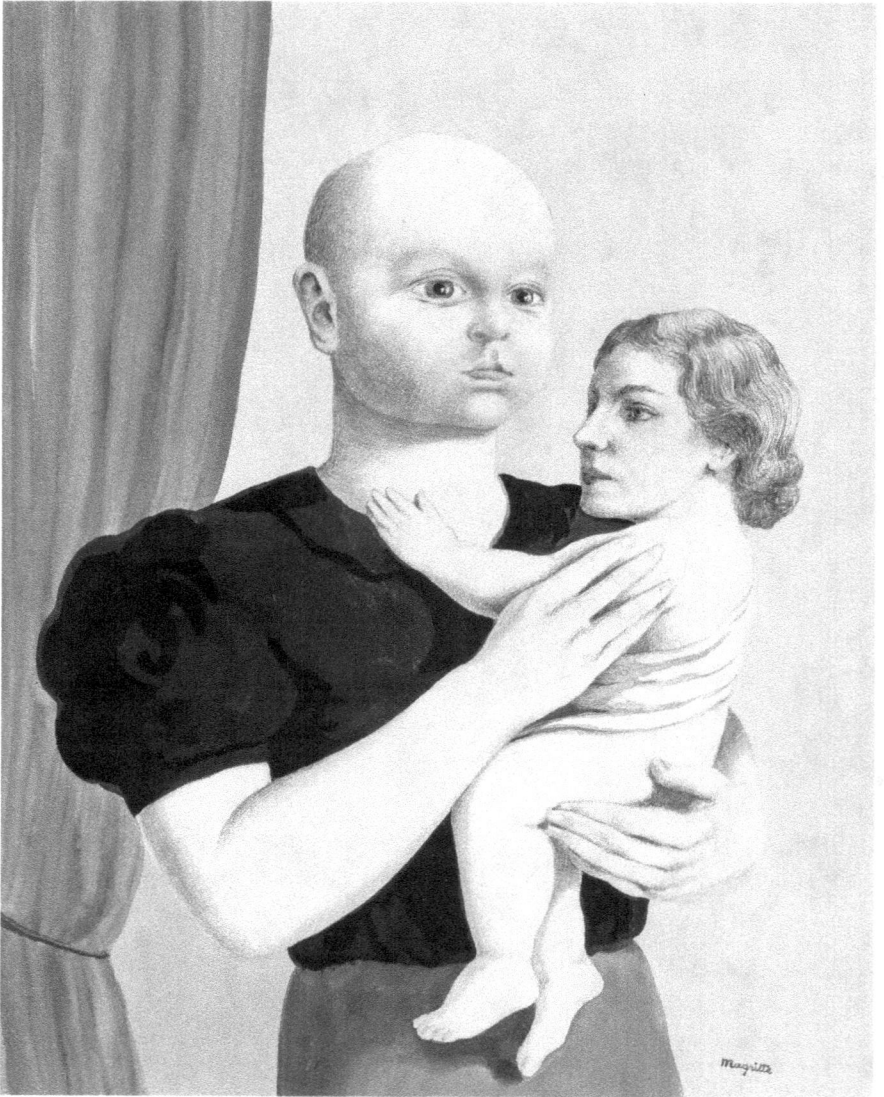

Chapter 7

Magritte and the Use of an Object

René Magritte's 1937 painting portrays a shrunken, mature woman held aloft by a rigid, imposing child. Their exchanged heads and inverted places produce a chilling effect. Originally calling it *Maternity*, Magritte later enigmatically renamed the painting *The Spirit of Geometry*. Perhaps, like geometry, the image explores the size, shape, position, and dimensions of an intimately bounded relationship. But its perspective explodes what we expect from this relationship.

Magritte's own childhood in Belgium was famously marred by his father's drunkenness and mother's suicide. Faced with poverty as an adult during the Second World War, he resorted to the forgery of banknotes. "I live in a very unpleasant world because of its routine ugliness," Magritte confessed in an interview in 1947, "That's why my painting is a battle, or rather a counter-offensive. The world is so strange. And can we ever know the world?"[1]

Typical of the Surrealist movement with which Magritte's work aligned, at least until he parted ways with the more anarchic Parisian branch, the unsettling image disrupts commonsense perceptions of what is actual. The Surrealists were notoriously fractious and contentious—fist fights erupted between authors of rival manifestos—but, as a whole, they shared a sensibility influenced by Freud's writings on free association, dream analysis, and unconscious life.

In 1924, André Breton, who trained in psychiatry and experimented with psychoanalytic methods treating shell-shocked combat soldiers, authored what is regarded as the most influential Surrealist manifesto. In it, he recalls how, just before falling asleep one evening, he perceived a distinct voice uttering "a rather strange phrase ... so clearly articulated" there could be absolutely no doubt as to what was said. The phrase—*"There is a man cut*

DOI: 10.4324/9781003536246-8

in two by the window"—accompanied by a "faint visual image," astonished him. It was, he writes, as if this imagistic phrase was "knocking at the window."[2]

Breton believed his vision was but one example of "the *superior* reality of certain forms of previously neglected associations" and "the omnipotence of dream." By portraying that superior reality, the Surrealist vision has the power, he concludes somewhat grandiosely, to "ruin once and for all other psychic mechanisms and to substitute itself for them in solving all the principal problems of life."[3]

It is notable that Breton, who might have been vicariously traumatized by the gruesome war stories to which he had been exposed, deemed his hypnogogic image representative of the "omnipotence" of unconscious dream life. Had Breton simply posited the omni*presence* of dream life, including in waking states, that would have been a different matter. But Breton stakes a claim for the all-powerful preeminence of dream life, which he claims expresses a "superior reality." The aim of Surrealism, many adherents concluded, was to foster the "triumphant reign of the pleasure principle" and thereby "undermine rational unity."[4]

But does Magritte's painting do that? Might there not be other ways of understanding what is at play in the bizarre juxtaposition of mother and child? While the image certainly undermines rational expectations, does it unequivocally substitute a triumphant pleasure principle for a reality principle?

Magritte, who was a prolific writer himself, actually framed the matter with greater subtlety. First of all, he believed art inherently resists psychoanalytic interpretation. Art, Magritte writes, "evokes the mystery without which the world would not exist." But, he says, "no one in his right mind believes psychoanalysis could elucidate the world's mystery."[5] Because psychoanalysis relates to everything as "a problem to be solved," he sarcastically adds, "perhaps psychoanalysis is itself the best subject to be treated by psychoanalysis."[6]

In addition, Magritte was keen to emphasize his work derived not from dreams but from "the mystery of everyday life."[7] Some might argue this is a distinction without a difference. But Magritte saw it otherwise. In a 1967 letter to the art historian Volker Nahmen, he insisted the word "dream" be cut from reference to his work because "the dream is *sub*-reality—that is, there is nothing poetic about it." Magritte saw his paintings as *sur*real, a form of "visual poetry," which gives "a sense of passion to reality we have found to be inadequate."[8] "The surreal," Magritte repeatedly noted, "is not to be confused with the desire for an imaginary world"—by which he means the world of dreams and unconscious phantasy. Instead, the project of Surrealism is one of "stripping" reality "of the banal ... meaning attached to it." The surreal, Magritte concludes, "is reality which has not been separated from its mystery."[9]

How might we understand what Magritte has in mind? It seems to me Magritte is grappling with how to speak about artistic creations without being constrained by Freud's two principles of mental functioning—the pleasure of phantasy and demands of reality. He does not deny art draws upon wellsprings of unconscious life. But Surrealism—or at least his understanding of it—involves a process other than the projection and "triumph" of wish-fulfilling phantasy *over* reality. Art occupies a space that partakes of, but is "something more" than, concrete actuality. By stripping away conventional modes of apprehension, there is leeway to "bring a sense of passion to reality" and see the familiar in a surprisingly unfamiliar light. "We must go in search of enchantment," Magritte famously declared, "revealing the unknown quality in each object."[10]

"Enchantment" is the work of the imaginative enlivening "banal" or conventional reality. Through idiosyncratic juxtaposition and interplay of the literal and figurative, it draws upon an unconscious subtext even as it elaborates and gives meaning to the text itself. Magritte's paintings often place ordinary objects in unexpected contexts or combinations so as to shake loose the habitual; the viewer beholds the inanimate, cold world afresh. Through what might be called an unfurling of imaginative capacities—both the artist's and the beholder's—hidden possibilities emerge. The enchantment of the imaginative is Magritte's "counter-offensive" against the "routine ugliness" of the banal or concrete world.

At the same time, however, Magritte repeatedly cautions the viewer to beware of the "treachery" of images.[11] It is as if he is keen to remind us that in art, as in life, both meanings of illusion are simultaneously in play: Alongside the vitalizing work of the imaginative, where the dichotomy between fact and phantasy need not yet figure, lurks the deceptive lure of the illusory. Is it possible not to conflate them? At what point does "mystery" become mystification?

In the 1990s, the Winnicott scholar Jan Abram saw Magritte's painting in a newspaper review of an upcoming London exhibition. Beneath the image, the reviewer had added the words: "KEEPING MUM." Abram found the image, together with the caption, "breathtaking." She readily saw Magritte's painting as a portrayal of Winnicott's theory of early psychic trauma and as emblematic of what she calls "the intrapsychic non-surviving object."[12]

Terror is an affect that, according to Abram, arises as a consequence of profound disturbance of maternal care. Building upon Winnicott's ideas regarding the "use of an object," Abram posits that it is the mother's capacity to reliably survive the infant's primitive benign aggression that allows the infant to place the object in the outside world. "This emotional achievement," writes Abram, "means the subject starts to be able to perceive the object as separate and differentiated."[13]

I'd like to offer a different, although compatible, perspective. I am prompted to do so because of a single sentence in Winnicott's seminal paper. It is at the point in the paper in which he has already described how the subject first "relates to" and then "destroys" the object, and that the object may or may not "survive" being destroyed. Here, of course, is the root of Abram's ideas about the surviving and non-surviving object. But Winnicott goes on to say that "a new feature thus arrives in the theory of object relating."[14] Describing this *new* feature, Winnicott adds, in italics, the particular sentence that caught my attention: "*This is the difficult part of my thesis, at least for me.*"[15] What idea is it, exactly, that Winnicott finds hard to accept?

It cannot possibly be about the object surviving ruthless aggression, for there was nothing new about that idea for him. He had been writing along those lines for decades. It shows up in his paper on primitive emotional development 20 years earlier and in his theory of the transitional object, which, he notes, must "survive instinctual loving and hating and, if it be a feature, pure aggression."[16] Having repeatedly established that mothers and analysts must survive early "instinctual love" or "ruthless" appetitive aggression, there had to be something else problematic for him to accept.

I suspect it was this: Winnicott surprised himself in that he was *fundamentally* redescribing the nature and origin of the two principles of mental functioning and, with them, Freud's dual instinct theory. The problem had been nagging at him for quite some time. Beginning in the 1950s, he had written about the infant's "motility impulses"—the self-directed, non-defensive movement of the organism *beginning in utero*—as bringing about "a discovery of environment, this latter being the opposition that is met through movement, and sensed during movement."[17] The motility impulse is *aggressive* in that it *"needs to find opposition … needs some-thing to push against."*[18] The infant begins to discover a world of objects by physically pushing against them. But, as the "psyche and soma aspects" of the growing infant "gradually … become distinguishable,"[19] there is also an *imaginative elaboration of the psychosomatic experience.* Here begins the experience of illusion in which a spontaneous gesture arising "out of need and by impulse" *creates* the objects that are found.[20] Imaginative movement now accompanies physical motility. But, while it might be said that there is then "*contact* … between psyche and the environment,"[21] there is not yet, at this stage, *an experience* of externality. A world created out of need vanishes when need dissipates. In Winnicott's language, the baby is only "feeding on the self."[22]

Something new needs to occur for the baby to feed from an other-than-me source. As early as 1948, Winnicott understood that a gradual process of disillusionment plays an important part.[23] The reality principle, he repeatedly reminds us, is an inevitable "insult."[24] But he was not content with the idea that reality is only something imposed upon the infant; that recognition of externality is solely contingent upon frustration and disillusionment. Has the infant no contribution of its own to make? Had not the baby's motility impulse always sought out and found pleasure in bumping up against objects?

Winnicott worked this problem over and over again. In fact, he repeatedly delayed publication of his book *Human Nature* because, as he wrote in a note attached to the final typescript, he could not bring himself to publish it until "the matter resolved itself, for me, in 'The Use of an Object.'"[25] What resolves the matter is the surprising insight he comes to when, finally, he "examines the reality principle under high power."[26]

A robust experience of externality, Winnicott concludes, arises out of the infant's imaginative repudiation of their own caretaker. Earlier, the child had enjoyed *appropriating*, pressing their body into, taking from, and greedily devouring. Now, they imaginatively do the opposite: They find relief in *repudiating*, pushing her away, "ridding" themself of her.[27] It is as if Winnicott turns the Garden of Eden story on its head! The infant aggressively banishes mother from the safety of their commingled state. But, unlike with appetitive desire whereby the world "vanishes" because need dissipates, the infant is now imagining mother continuing to exist, only "elsewhere." But *where* is that elsewhere? And what is "elsewhere" *imagined to be like?*

Winnicott adheres as best he can to the infant's point of view, trying to imagine what the infant imagines. The not-me "elsewhere" is a potentially dangerous territory, a no-man's land, which the child does not yet know can sustain life. Winnicott poignantly describes this as "experimenting with excursions over the line into the *wasteland* of destroyed reality."[28]

T.S. Eliot's *The Waste Land* was, of course, widely regarded in Winnicott's time as one of the most important poems of the 20th century. In the first of its five sections, "The Burial of the Dead," T.S. Eliot asks:

> what branches grow
> Out of this stony rubbish?

And answers:

> You cannot say, or guess, for you know only
> A heap of broken images, where the sun beats,
> And the dead tree gives no shelter, the cricket no relief,
> And the dry stone no sound of water …
> I will show you fear in a handful of dust.[29]

The child imaginatively relegates mother to a barren wilderness, leaving her there unprotected to fend for herself. He does so not angrily or vindictively, out of frustration, but *destructively for his own growth*. At great risk, the previous image he had in his mind—mother as an omnipotently controlled "subjective object"—is actively shattered. From the "heap of broken images," a new imaginative relationship with what is actual has the potential to emerge. "Destruction plays its part," concludes Winnicott, "in making the reality."[30]

In the little time remaining before his death, Winnicott continued to wrestle with how to understand the nature of the impulse that created an individuated experience of externality. Absorbing the comments and commentaries of his colleagues, he acknowledged that "it is this idea of a destructive first impulse that is difficult to grasp and I see that all this may have some flaw in it."[31] But the more he turned it over in his mind, the more it felt right to leave behind "something that we [psychoanalysts] have come to accept": The notion that development involves the fusion of the Life and Death instincts or, in its Kleinian iteration, Love and Hate. In its place, Winnicott is drawn to the idea that "the first drive is itself *one* thing, something I call 'destruction,' but I could have called ... a combined love–strife drive."[32] And, to drive the point home, he goes on to reiterate, this time in italics, "*It has nothing to do with anger at the inevitable frustrations associated with the reality principal*" because "the urge is not a pleasure–pain principle phenomenon."[33]

Appreciating he was in uncharted terrain, Winnicott grasps for an analogy: Mythological accounts of fire-breathing serpents and dragons cited by a 1st-century Roman naturalist. A significant portion of Pliny the Elder's *Naturalis Historia* pays tribute to the various powers of fire. Winnicott attributes to Pliny the question: "Who can say whether in essence fire is constructive or destructive?"*[34]

It is impossible to know whether Winnicott was fully cognizant of the import of the particular analogy he stumbled upon. Prometheus stealing fire and bestowing it upon humankind is the foundational myth for the ancient Greek understanding of the imaginative. The name Prometheus, meaning "fore-sight," designates "the power to anticipate the future by projecting an horizon of imaginary possibilities."[35] Zeus, of course, famously punishes Prometheus by chaining him to a rock and sending an eagle to devour his liver. But what is at the root of the horrible transgression warranting such wrath? It is this: By harnessing the power of this stolen fire, mortals "transmuted the order of nature (the cosmos of blind necessity governed by Zeus) into the order of culture (a realm of relative freedom ...)."[36] The fire Prometheus gave mortals was both literal and figurative—the flames of combustion and the sparks of the imaginative. By acquiring the imaginative realm, mortals made themselves into demigods, inventing worlds of their own and discovering the "metaphysical distinction between what happens to us, and what we make of this happening."[37]

The Irish literary critic Denis Donoghue saw Prometheus as providing humankind with "the transformation grammar of experience" and "a sense of the endlessness of possibility arising from the endlessness of knowledge and desire." These imaginative capacities, he notes, have "always been a contentious power."[38] Plato and Aristotle famously feuded over them, the former wanting to censure and banish images from the Republic because they were "false," and the later celebrating their positive role as intermediaries in the search for what is "true."[39] Here, again, the two faces of illusion.

---

* As far as I have been able to discern, this is a paraphrasing of Pliny rather than an actual quote.

And so Winnicott—wittingly or unwittingly—returns us to the realm of the imaginative as a primary unitary drive at the root of the psyche. Imaginative elaboration is what the psyche does, beginning with the body's physical aliveness, eventually generating increasingly complex experiences of externality, and from there "transmuting the order of nature … into the order of culture." Without imaginative elaboration, nothing "meaningful" can be experienced, no distinction drawn between "what happens to us, and what we make of this happening." For any "happening" to have personal *meaning*, there needs to be a simultaneous *appropriation*—moving toward an object, claiming and making something of it for myself—and an equally opposite *repudiation*—distinguishing me from not-me, separating one possibility from another, a foreclosure of other meanings. The primary drive, the work of the imaginative, does both.

But, as Donoghue reminds us, these imaginative capacities have "always been a contentious power." Prometheus's act was an affront, a provocation. Winnicott, too, remarks that what he terms "destruction" could just as easily have been called "provocation." "Perhaps the right word," Winnicott adds, "has not been found."[40]

Who's to say if the imaginative is constructive or destructive? For Winnicott, the answer hinges on the caretaker's capacity to survive the creative/destructive upheaval of appropriation and repudiation. Even a god such as Zeus, Donoghue reminds us, can be what Abram calls a "non-surviving object," punishing rather than welcoming the human impulse to imaginatively appropriate and repudiate.

In light of all this, it is worth returning to Magritte's image, which captures something of *what it feels like* when the "spirit of geometry"—the necessary differences between how and when generations care for each other—is violated.

Through whose angle of vision is the world perceived? Which one is the parent, and which the child? Who is "supporting" whom? Magritte's surreal image jarringly depicts something true about distortions in development that can arise from such violation. Both mother and child exist in a hardened and petrified state.

From one point of view, this may be the affect of terror, identified by Abram as the catastrophic consequence of the child's experience of a needed adult's failure to survive the emotional demands of caretaking. In states of vulnerability, there is no one for the child to safely depend on. The absence of reliable understanding between mother and child creates a world devoid of basic trust. And a world without basic trust is, indeed, terrifying.

Terror, though, may not be the only thing we see in these transfixed and benumbed images. These figures have lost a connection to their own imaginative aliveness. They are petrified in the same way organic matter can become encrusted and ossified. The world they inhabit is known only in its literal concreteness, with little, if any, access to the imaginative aliveness necessary to transform disillusionment and grievance into meaningful grief.

Enid Balint offers the useful idea that such a state results from the caretaker's imperviousness. The child cannot find an "echo" of himself coming from an Other. He thereby hollows out, becoming "empty" of himself.[41] Kenneth Wright calls the mother's imperviousness "the 'look' of the Gorgon," which turns the child into stone.[42]

A child like this has no meaningful rapport with external reality because they are unable to contribute imaginatively to the creation of that reality. Mother's point of view obliterates their own. As they scan the world, mother's needs so overwhelm their natural rhythm of engaging and withdrawing that what is external comes to be experienced only as something to contend with rather than used imaginatively as a medium for self-discovery.

Mother's unpredictability and fragility overwhelm and stunt the child's nascent capacity to imaginatively repudiate her. The child dare not banish her to the "wasteland of destroyed reality." How could mother possibly survive in it? How can the child risk placing her *out there*? With the child psychically compelled to keep her close so she can survive, mother and child become entombed, the child's sacrifice carrying the unconscious hope of keeping her alive. Haunted by mother's desolate and impoverished imaginings, the child is unable to be safely alone with their own.

This child cannot afford to do what is necessary for their own growth: Imaginatively repudiate and release her, find a way to be in a world that is disclaimed, make the world into a life-enhancing possibility, use their imaginative capacities to transform vague hopes into effective desire.

With the child's voracious appetitive love they worry: How can mother survive *me*? With their need to repudiate and cast mom off, they agonize: How can mother survive *without me*?

Unable to either appropriate or repudiate, the child's felt-sense of external reality becomes one of a grotesque, abject, and "meaningless armature."[43] What is actual might be experienced concretely or delusionally, but not imaginatively. The landscape is one of debilitating doubt and corrosive credulity that cannot shimmer.

Chapter 8

Are We Virtuoso Storytellers?

In 1866, after fighting with Garibaldi in the Third Italian War of Independence, the painter Achille Glisenti opened an antiquarian gallery in Florence. In his vintage etching *The Hunter's Tale*, Glisenti portrays an archetypal scene of storytelling, reminiscent of Carlo Ginzburg's contention that huntsmen's prehistoric narratives lie at the root of human society (see Chapter 2). One need not hear words spoken to know a tale is being told.

The facial expressions of the people gathered around the table suggest the story is heard differently by each of them. Perhaps their varied reactions are related to what it feels like imagining themselves in whatever scene the huntsman is describing, how his animated manner of storytelling affects them, or their personal relationship with the teller of the tale.

The literary scholar Richard Kearney believes storytelling—the dramatic plotting of human action—is a communicative act that creates a shareable world. "Every story," Kearney notes, "no matter the genre, style, voice or plot, shares a common function of someone telling something to someone about something."[1] Even the solipsistic monologues of Samuel Beckett's fractured postmodern characters are ultimately addressed to an implicit other.

From a psychoanalytic point of view, it is by no means evident who that "implicit other" might be. Communicative acts are often unconsciously intended for figures real and imagined, present or not. Transference is predicated on the idea that people continually reinvent the person to whom they are speaking. It is always worth wondering for whose benefit a story is being told.

Kearney, who approaches storytelling from a literary point of view, claims that "every life is in search of a narrative."[2] We seek these narratives, Kearney concludes, "to introduce some kind of concord into the everyday

DOI: 10.4324/9781003536246-9

discord and dispersal we find about us."[3] But, through storytelling, we also address the disarray we find *within us*. Haphazard happenings are transformed into intelligible events by virtue of their rendering in the form of a story. While storytelling is ostensibly communicative, it is no less a stay against confusion, a medium through which intolerable psychic pain is imaginatively transformed into more bearable forms of suffering. As such, the question arises: Are we, or must we be, virtuoso storytellers?

A chorus of contemporary voices places narrative at the heart of self-experience. Jerome Bruner, among the pioneers of the so-called "narrative turn" in psychology, says the Self is perpetually engaged in rewriting its own story,[4] and that we eventually "become the autobiographical narratives by which we 'tell about' our lives."[5] Or, as the philosopher Charles Taylor puts it: "Our lives exist in a space of questions, which only a coherent narrative can answer."[6]

There are even those, such as the literary critic Peter Brooks, who claim narrative is fundamental to our sense of reality. "We don't simply arrange random facts into narratives," he writes, but "our sense of the way stories go together, how life is made meaningful as narrative, presides at our choice of facts as well, and the ways we present them."[7] Brooks upends Ginzburg's evidential paradigm: We didn't merely evolve to arrange facts into a narrative arc. Our preferred narrative arc determines which facts we choose to arrange. And we select facts to ensure our narratives cohere. If you deprive people of coherent stories, says Alasdair MacIntyre, "you leave them unscripted, anxious stutterers in their actions as in their words."[8]

Whether crafting an argument, telling a well-wrought story, or re-presenting our lives, we use narrative to generate aesthetic distance from which to view events, transform facts into meaningful personal know-ledge, and obtain a measure of relief from what is uncertain. Narrative thought imaginatively generates compelling dramas and believable, even if untrue, historical accounts. Fueled by our drive to endow experience with meaning, narrative imagination, George Eliot claimed, is "the nearest thing to life."[9]

Narrative imagination may be "the nearest thing to life," but it can also be employed to evade unpalatable truths about life. "Can I lie here and side step some memory I'd rather not entertain," asks the Irish author Dermot Healy, "and then let fiction take care of it elsewhere?" "Fiction," Healy says, "becomes the receptacle for those truths we would rather not allow into our tales of the self."[10] Do fiction and non-fiction ever fully part ways, especially if reality needs to be narratively imagined to even register? Through narrative, lived experience is given leeway to roam into possible worlds.

No wonder psychoanalysis, to borrow from MacIntyre, remains a somewhat anxious stutterer on this question of narrative, with pendulum swings punctuating both the history of the profession and individual treatments. Narrative involves an account of a series of related events or experiences. But what does it mean to say events constitute a series or are related? When are narrative coherence and continuity welcome features, and when troublesome impediments? How do we distinguish narrative truth from historical truth?[11] And what does a "story," let alone an account of a story, look like *before* there are words?

"The mind is such a new place," Emily Dickinson once wrote to a friend, "last night feels obsolete."[12] Dickinson, a poet finely attuned to inner inconsistencies, no doubt knew herself as a continuous ongoing being. She nevertheless marveled at how transient her states of mind could be and balked at rendering a consistent story of herself.

Ralph Waldo Emerson was similarly struck by the discontinuities of his lived experience. It puzzles him how, one day, everything feels dreary and vacuous and he cannot write a word while, on the next, he is full of thoughts and finds it the most natural thing to write as he pleases. And, when he then looks back on what he has written, he wonders who it could possibly have been that "wrote so many continuous pages." "Our moods," Emerson concludes, "do not believe in each other."[13]

"The other one, the one called Borges, is the one things happen to," writes Jorge Luis Borges. Borges knows of this "other Borges" from the mail that arrives and from seeing his name in biographical dictionaries. The relationship between the two of them is not exactly hostile but it is, nevertheless, a rather curious and strained one. Borges is acutely aware of Borges the storyteller's "perverse custom" of dissimulating and magnifying things. Indeed, sometimes he recognizes himself more in other people's stories than in the ones written by the writer known as Borges. Besides, what Borges—whoever he may be—writes doesn't really belong to either of them. Once written, it belongs "to the language and to tradition."[14]

Henry James echoed Borges's experience of the otherness of himself in a letter to his brother, William. Responding to criticism William raised about his novel *The Europeans*, James said he thought of the book as "the work of quite another person than myself." This "other person" is "a rich relation … who suffers me still to claim a shy fourth cousinship." James believes that, so long as he treats this distant cousin with decency and gratitude and "keeps him in good humor," he will surely "do great things for me." The cousin is "a very agreeable relation," James concludes, *"But I am not him."*[15]

Like Borges, Henry James can be seen as slyly distancing himself from accountability and agency. The story he's telling—about a shy fourth cousin—disowns any enduring autobiographical narrative. Even his talent as a writer is presented as residing "elsewhere." It is this distant cousin who does great things. One wonders if perhaps a part of him feels "shy" about the successful author he has become.

But James's seeming evasion also communicates something real: The novel, in a certain sense, was not written by the same "Henry James" who communicates with his brother. The novelist in him is at least partially dissociated from who he feels himself to be in other contexts. The seeming self-sameness of the embodied "Henry James" is hard to reconcile with the transient flux of his experiencing "I." Nor does it easily align with the strange "otherness" of unconscious life, which is why writers often experience inspiration as coming from "elsewhere." Furthermore, the English language James speaks is thoroughly "populated" and saturated with the meanings and intentions of those who came before the person known as "Henry James."[16] James is embedded in a particular culture the tool kit of which is not of his own making. As Borges said, what he's written belongs not to himself but to the language and the tradition.

No matter how it might appear from an external point of view, the "story" of one's life is inevitably filtered through a particular temporal temperament, a dispositional rhythm of moving between discontinuous states of mind. Individuals, and even cultures, differ markedly in how they oscillate between what is felt to be transient and what is experienced as enduring. Some find greater meaning in the former, and some in the latter. Tension between the transient and enduring often comes to the fore at moments of transition: A baby moving from sucking to chewing, a toddler learning to speak or to walk, an adult falling in love, leaving home, gazing at a first-born child, or losing their parents. At such junctures, it is common for a person to feel unrecognizable to themself.

There is good reason, therefore, to cast doubt on the reliability and import of autobiographical narrative. Bruner's claim that "we become the autobiographical narratives by which we 'tell about' our lives" is true only to the extent we remove or abstract ourselves from the discontinuous experiencing "I," look at ourselves as if from the "outside," and ignore all the otherness of unconscious life and cultural embeddedness. "One shouldn't write one autobiography," says the French analyst J.-B. Pontalis, "but ten or a hundred because, while we have only one life we have innumerable ways of recounting that life to ourselves."[17] As James Wood points out, in any story there is a *"surplus of life* trying to get beyond the death" imposed by any author as they choose how the story is told and when the story ends.[18]

We all need a measure of respite from the surplus of life. Stories, and narrative coherence more generally, provide such relief even as they carry the risk of seducing us into comforting artificiality. The short-story writer and novelist Robert Boswell sees this seduction at play across the landscape of commercial America. The artifice of seemingly known stories substitutes for imaginatively lived experience. Popular franchises such as McDonald's and Disneyland are places where "expectations are carefully managed and our imaginations are kept in check." While they allow us to escape from the real world for a while, they are not "places where we can truly experience life."[19]

Boswell believes the same to be true of the stereotypic characters presented on commercial TV. They provide a measure of comfort precisely because they display a reliable repetition of a patterned narrative. A stereotype, Boswell notes, "is any character that is fully known"[20] and *"to make something fully known, is to make it unreal."*[21] If Boswell is right, it poses a challenge to the psychoanalytic call to "know thyself." One might very well need to "unknow" oneself so as to grow. We are prone all too readily to become caricatures of ourselves. For Boswell, "keeping imagination in check" provides relief but prevents us from "truly experiencing life."

Freud's view was capacious enough to hold in play seemingly opposing views on the nature of psychoanalytic storytelling. In "Constructions in Analysis," he paints an image of the analyst as a reliable narrator curing patients through coherent and comprehensive narratives. "What we are in search of," writes Freud, "is a picture of the patient's forgotten years that shall be alike trustworthy and in all essential respects complete."[22] The patient, in this version, is an unreliable narrator with a "tell," unwittingly revealing himself through symptoms. Freud's approach, as Adam Phillips puts it, is to "trust the untold tale, not the teller."[23]

The medium through which the untold tale emerges is believed to be that of transference, which Freud elsewhere calls an "intermediate region," both real and imaginative, "between illness and real life."[24] In the "artificial" playground of transference, the analyst must, in Peter Brooks's gloss, help the patient construct a more coherent narrative, one "whose syntax and rhetoric are more convincing, more adequate to give an interpretative account of the story of the past," than what previously had been presented in symptomatic form.[25]

Although Freud was masterful at organizing patients' associations, dreams, and memories into persuasive and seemingly conclusive narratives, he also allows an opposing current to hold sway. Conceding that what emerges in treatment "can be inaccurate but sufficient,"[26] he gestures toward a more fictional account of psychoanalytic storytelling.

In fact, given Freud's understanding of memory, what emerges in analysis is *inevitably* inaccurate. "The essential elements of an experience," he writes in a paper on screen memories, "are represented in memory by the inessential elements of the same experience."[27] Through imaginative acts of substitution and displacement, childhood is made retrospectively bearable. We create, in other words, shabby cover stories, akin to waking dreams. And, as Freud considered the stories we tell ourselves in this light, he questioned whether "we have any memories at all *from* our childhood; memories related *to* our childhood may be all that we possess."[28] Freud, in search of a picture "that shall be alike trustworthy and ... complete," was at the same time suspicious of narratives—his patients' and his own—presented as unassailable documentary evidence.

Freud's "procedure of free association and so on is queer," Ludwig Wittgenstein once remarked, because he "never shows how we know where to stop—where is the right solution." Sometimes, Freud claims the correct analysis "is the one which satisfies the patient." But, at other times, he asserts that only the analyst "knows what the right ... analysis of the dream is, whereas the patient doesn't." How Freud decides which analysis is correct, Wittgenstein concludes, "does not seem to be a matter of evidence."[29]

What Wittgenstein found "queer" about psychoanalysis was the paradox that Freud's method of free association—which by its very nature has no end point—was employed as a treatment designed to reach a clear narrative conclusion. Wittgenstein, it seems, intuited a contradiction between two co-existing views of unconscious life. In one version, it was a repository of repressed memories amenable to translation into a coherent narrative. But no less salient was the understanding of unconscious life as an incessant form of "deep dreaming ... at the core of the personality,"[30] irrepressibly subverting conscious coherence; a force Malcolm Bowie refers to as "unstoppable transformational processes"[31] that "prevent[s] meaning from reaching fullness, completion, closure, consummation."[32] This other version of unconscious life—the part of ourselves always undermining our own narrative—is one of a perpetually disruptive organization evoking the potential to either traumatize or generatively experience things afresh.

Narrative coherence—and coherent explanations—can be a defensive gambit. "Free association that reveals a coherent theme," writes Winnicott, "is already affected by anxiety, and the cohesion of ideas is a defense organization."[33] Often this derives from too vigilant a need for self-holding, a precipitate foreclosure of the imaginative freedom to drift about and enter non-purposive states that aren't yet built up into a coherent version of a self. And yet it is precisely the loss of a capacity to make coherent sense of one's predicament that is a hallmark of trauma.

Here, then, is an inherent difficulty: Narrative coherence is a necessary solution and a recurring problem. In accordance with the evidential paradigm, it facilitates successful adaptation to the actual world. Without it, we risk being chaotically traumatized. But, in accordance with the "unstoppable" transformations of "deep dreaming," narrative coherence potentially hinders aliveness. An assiduously unified and consistent narrative is often a regrettable sign of bad faith and inauthenticity into which we are seduced. From the first point of view, the aim of psychoanalysis is to generate a more coherent account of our lives. But, from the other, it is to live on better terms with the deep dreaming process that perpetually disrupts our coherence.

From a developmental point of view, narrative coherence is an achievement realized within a particular environment, not a given. Winnicott suggests that, well before speech, physiological rhythms, "inherent in existence," need to come to their natural "completion." These physiological processes are also part of an infant's psychology, and, if mother fails to hold the situation in time, baby experiences a disturbing state of "non-completion."[34] Adults, too, are intimately familiar with what it feels like to be "interrupted." The subjective sense of non-completion suggests some intuitive sense of what constitutes a "total happening," a trajectory with a beginning, middle, and an end. Is there something akin to an inherent narrative arc built into desire and experience?

The developmental psychologist Daniel Stern suggests infants are hardwired to parse and chunk into a narrative format the stimulations with which they are bombarded. The narrative format—"a structure for mentally organizing (without language) our experience with motivated human behavior"—is designed to build meaning around intentions.[35] Although of relatively short duration, occurrences that are narratively formatted become "a special kind of story … lived as it happens, not as it is put in to words afterwards."[36] Every present moment created in the here and now—Virginia Woolf called them "moments of being"[37]—contains within its brief existence "a lived story,"[38] a "sort of untold emotional narrative."[39]

While employing different language, both Winnicott and Stern suggested that some process unit with duration is needed to make sense of experiences as they unfold in real time. And that the sensitivity of caretakers to these inherent processes—allowing them to take their natural course—is crucial to well-being.

Chaotic, threatening, and negligent environments traumatize because they disrupt or warp the child's "untold emotional narrative." An accretion of impingements upon the natural unfolding of a child's lived stories makes it difficult later on for the traumatized individual to construct a believable story about themselves with a place in the world. They are robbed of the measure of psychosomatic integration and psychic equilibrium necessary for creating coherent accounts of experience which they, themselves, can find believable and true.

No wonder it is often difficult to follow the narratives of traumatized individuals. The conventional scaffolding of narrative arc—a beginning, a middle, an end—often goes missing. Analysts find themselves inclined to "fill in the gaps" or irritably inquire with the hope that the story told becomes more readily "understandable."

Adults who went through phases of elective mutism as children have much to teach in this regard. They often recall their earlier silence as a state in which they were generating more meaning than they knew what to do with. At any given moment, the competition for salience turns an excess of arousal into meaningless noise. There is no clear signal they can "wrap their mind around." Unable to say everything, they end up saying nothing. They are painfully aware that any story always produces more stories. "A story," says James Wood, "is story- producing."[40] The elective mute cannot select among them because they are preoccupied with the seemingly infinite untold stories of every incident that occurs. Put differently: From a subjective point of view, there is no "experience." A breakdown in the capacity to imaginatively elaborate—necessary for transforming "happenings" into delineated experience—prevents the structuring of thoughts into coherent and intelligible sequences felt by the individual as an expression of a personal self. Eventually, the mind can even go vacant.

"Humankind," wrote T. S. Eliot, "cannot bear very much reality."[41] A vast psychoanalytic literature concurs that there is always more "reality" than the mind can possibly contain.[42] Only a small portion of sensorial arousal—little shocks to the system—undergoes the kind of imaginative elaboration that allows narrative meaning to emerge. The lateralized hemispheres of the brain, with their distinct modes of apprehension and deployment of attention, appear implicated in the ongoing inner struggle to generate a semblance of narrative "coherence."[43] But there remains an inevitable gap between raw sensorial arousals apprehended globally and what can be imaginatively fashioned into coherent narrative. And it is worth wondering: What happens to the excess?

Narrative coherence acts as a shock absorber, providing a measure of relief from the stark immediacy of arousals, unpredictability of what is not yet known, and inchoate awareness of that "something more" or "something else" that remains beyond the formulation of experience. Some minds are shocked more than others, some environments do not allow stories to unfold, and some stories can never be told.

Much occurs, to borrow from the title of Enid Balint's collected papers, "Before I Was I."[44] We certainly don't start out with any settled sense of "I," "Me," or "You." While quietly alert, a normal healthy baby has no idea they are the same being who earlier had been excitedly nursing. Nor are they aware that their beleaguered nervous system in distress "resides within" a "me" who will be there later in a relaxed state of mind. It takes a fair amount of time for these islands of dissociated states to link up and cohere somewhat. While there may be an inherent developmental push toward integration, it is perfectly natural to drift among dissociated states, each state carrying a reality, and a "story," all its own.[45]

Just as a newborn cannot be aware they are the self same individual immersed in the warm sensations of a bath as the one in the throes of a powerful urge to attack mother's body, they do not know that mother is the same mother in each of these situations. Only gradually do they build up images that remain relatively coherent and stable across discontinuous realities.

"Object constancy" is the name generally given to this capacity to maintain stable images across emotional states. It is no small achievement to conceive of another person existing even when out of sight and retain a felt sense of their positive attributes even in states of dissatisfaction. Once object constancy is achieved, attachment becomes relatively independent of gratification or frustration, and the transitions between fluctuating states of mind become more fluid and bearable.

But object constancy entails far more than simply recalling episodic memories of figures across situations. It presumes a built-up rudimentary "I" that simultaneously "holds" dramatically discontinuous mind states. Daniel Stern coined the term RIGS—representations of interactions that have been generalized—to describe "the basic unit for the representation of the core self."[46] RIGS are abstracted, distilled prototypes or composite images based on repeated episodes of self–other–affect encounters. Over time, these "generalized" interactions "stand in" for all the other actual ones. "Whenever a RIG of being with someone ... is activated," writes Stern, "an infant encounters an evoked companion."[47] Stern's RIGS point to a realm of palpable experience enriched by, but also beyond, the mere memory of evidential facts. A *composite* image, *evoking* a companion, *stands in* for the veridical memory of actual encounters. RIGS, while based on actual experiences, are *potential* images, not veridical recollections.

At the very "core" of the Self, Stern seems to imply, a rudimentary imaginative process is in play. And, for there to be object constancy, the "basic units" of Stern's "core self"—which themselves are distilled images of interactions—must engage in something other than mere recall. That "something other" is an imaginative act. A baby's rudimentary "I" intuits a connection beyond the immediacy of stimulus-bound experience. Children imaginatively create a bridge between the perceptually present reality and one that exists "elsewhere." Somewhere beyond the immediacy of a "hateful me-her-stabbing-pain, which I can see, hear, feel, and touch" is a "loving me-her-pleasurable sensation that my senses cannot presently detect." What we call object constancy (which is a foundation of hope) involves, in other words, imaginative processes potentially freeing a person from stimulus-bound reactivity. Something of the imagined interaction blends into how the immediate one is experienced, the pain thus made more bearable. This does not mean imagined relief magically removes actual pain. But it does allow the pain to be suffered differently. Or, to put this another way: The imaginative turns unfathomable pain into fathomable, and thereby more containable, suffering.

The artist and AIDS activist Nan Goldin claims it is "always easier to make one's life into a story than it is to sustain real memories." "The real experience," Goldin says, "has a smell and is dirty and is not wrapped in simple endings." In memories, "things can appear that you didn't want to see. Where you are not safe." And, even if one fails to "unleash" these memories, "the effect is there. It is in your body."[48]

Goldin seems to endorse the view that the stories we tell are, as Freud suggested, shabby cover stories. Certain actual experiences—Goldin calls them "real"—come to be experienced as dissociatively "irreal." The situation was so unfathomable, the pain so great, that the person could only endure it by psychically removing themselves from their own experience.

Goldin also suggests that certain memories inscribe themselves in the body rather than register in the mind. The effect of their impact is there, even though recall is hazy or missing. Goldin subscribes to Bessel van der Kolk's notion that "the body keeps score."[49] But, if this is so, what kind of storytelling or translation is required to make the ledger intelligible? Can the story really be told? Who tells the tale, and what might get lost in the telling?

Cathy Caruth says trauma calls out for stories. The problem, however, is that what traumatically overwhelms—it "has a smell and is dirty and is not wrapped in simple endings"—cannot really be rendered as a story because it wasn't actually "experienced" at the time it occurred. There is, Caruth says, an inevitable "delay or incompletion in knowing."[50] Trauma, in her felicitous phrase, is an "unclaimed experience."[51] Winnicott calls this a "death that happened but was not experienced."[52] Traumatized individuals are possessed by intrusive images rather than being in possession of their own experience. The pain of shock, loss, and confusion cannot be imaginatively elaborated.

Caruth believes the traumatized person is forever needing to retrieve the "inexperienced experience" through narratives which re-present the original trauma in surrogate or vicarious form. But what inevitably thwarts imaginative elaboration and narrative rendering is the persistent "literality," the non-symbolic structure of traumatic symptoms which resist being fashioned into a story precisely because they remain literal.[53] Caruth believes it is the insistent return of this literality that constitutes the enigmatic core of trauma.

The traumatized individual, therefore, faces an impossible dilemma: For the "sake of testimony and for the sake of cure," a more imaginatively elaborated and integrated story needs to be told. The unfathomable must be made fathomable. But at, the same time, "the transformation of the trauma into a narrative memory that allows the story to be verbalized and communicated" means the "knowledge of the past may lose both the precision and the force" of the recalled trauma.[54]

And beyond the sacrifice of precision and force lies an even deeper cost: A violation of the incomprehensibility, the "*affront to understanding*,"[55] which is an essential element of the traumatic event. It is this violation, Caruth speculates, which underlies the reluctance of many traumatized individuals to speak of their experience. Rendering an incomprehensible trauma into an intelligible, stable story turns it into something inauthentic and counterfeit. No matter how well told—and perhaps even more so *if* well told—a story replaces the truth of the experience with what Claude Lanzmann calls "the absolute obscenity of understanding."[56] If there is a "story" in trauma, where does it reside?

It was Freud who first asked: "When does separation from an object produce anxiety, when does it produce mourning, and when does it produce, it may be, only pain?"[57] As is often the case, the question Freud asks is more interesting—in the sense of opening possibilities—than the answer he provides. What is striking about the choices Freud offers—anxiety, mourning, and pain—is that, despite his general emphasis on the need to relinquish wishful phantasy, separation from an actual other is viewed as a loss of momentous consequence. Even mourning, which from Freud's point of view "occurs under the influence of reality testing" and categorically demands of the bereaved a "detachment of libido," involves a greater degree of continuity of relationship than Freud acknowledges.[58] Attachments are far less interchangeable than Freud's theory of libido would suggest.

But even more telling than the range of emotional choices Freud highlights is his intriguing proposal that some experiences might involve *"only pain."* Pain—which involves a traumatic break in the stimulus barrier—is of an entirely different order than anxiety, frustration, or thwarted desire. What generates the earliest experiences of pain is the newborn's utter helplessness when separated from mother. Helplessness—and the traumatic pain that accompanies it—is, Freud tells us, the primordial condition of the human species. As an affective state, pain is not the result of a fantasized danger; it is a reaction appropriate to an actual loss. The immature psyche cannot contain, hold over time, or imaginatively elaborate pain.

In everyday language, words such as "pain" and "suffering" are used interchangeably to describe variations on our experience of being subjected to bad or unpleasant things. However, it is worth distinguishing between what are actually two dramatically different orders of experience. To give the simplest (and most concrete) of examples: Despite an array of mirror neurons, we don't actually *feel* someone else's physical pain. But we most certainly can share their suffering about their pain.

Pain, as Freud suggested, is a break in the stimulus barrier so concretely overwhelming as to be literally inaccessible to thought and feeling. Since the agony of pain is not represented in mind, it is as if it is from nowhere, exists everywhere, and has no meaning whatsoever. This kind of pain, however, is quite distinct from even the most horrible kinds of suffering. Suffering is pain made fathomable. Fathomable suffering is not *relief* from anguish. It doesn't make one "feel better." It does, however, make the agony more "bearable" in the sense that it is containable in mind, "thinkable," and, possibly, eventually available to be elaborated in ways that give the suffering a meaningful place in one's life.

Both Bion and Winnicott described how unelaborated pain is a different order of experiencing than elaborated suffering. For Bion, mother's absence engenders intolerable pain in an infant who has not yet developed a capacity to suffer.[59] Mother's terrifying absence is experienced as a "no-mother" or "no-breast," which the child is unable to process psychically. If mother—and this is a crucial "if"—can absorb or feel the fear, incomprehension, and loss *for* the infant, the agony now contained in mother's mind becomes less terrifying to the infant. Mother's emotional presence makes possible the child's growing tolerance of her physical separateness. A space in the infant's mind opens up where a dream thought—"no mother"—can exist. Where once there had been "just pain," there is now a symbolic mental presence of an absent mother, a symbolic image of "mother," and eventually a word, representing her.

"Imagination," says Cornelius Castoriadis, "is the power to represent that which is not."[60] What Bion adds, however, is that mother's imaginative empathy plays a role here. Mother's "reverie" facilitates the child's capacity to dream and thereby "represent that which is not." It is the imaginative work of dreaming that transfigures raw experiences into thoughts and transforms pain—a "nameless dread" devoid of meaning—into meaningful suffering.[61]

For Winnicott, too, suffering is a developmental achievement associated with imaginative elaboration of pain. Winnicott notes, for example, that the anguish, misery, and pain evident in mental hospitals is usually assessed in a "superficial way," and that "probably the greatest suffering in the human world" is actually "the suffering of normal or healthy or mature persons."[62] Winnicott does not mean to imply that the painful agony of people in mental hospitals is a "lesser" form of distress. He is highlighting that there are different orders and qualities of experiencing mental anguish. Suffering implies pain has been held and worked over in time, given a poignancy and depth absent in states of blunt or concrete pain. Suffering is fathomable—it carries meaning—where pain is not. Only when a hurt is recognized for what it actually is and imaginatively elaborated—held in time and felt in more ways than one—can it be suffered deeply and sorrowfully.

What, it might rightly be asked, does all this have to do with storytelling? In psychoanalysis, it is assumed that putting words to wounds carries the potential to transform the painfully actual into the imaginatively sufferable. Bion's "dreaming" and Winnicott's "imaginative elaboration" are steps toward making an experience fathomable. Narrative is the further formulation and articulation of the fathomable.

Nevertheless, there is no escaping the poignant paradox suggested by Caruth and Lanzmann: An imaginative elaboration is required for traumatic pain to feel real in a way that can be suffered. But rendering the incomprehensible into a stable, coherent story runs the risk of turning it into something counterfeit, if not "obscene." Words imply a measure of distance from an original shock, a loss, that is, of the actual immediate experience. Stories are symbolic substitutes tasked with resurrecting a moment or connection that is also being mourned. That is why we need to be virtuoso storytellers, even if the real story is one that cannot be told.

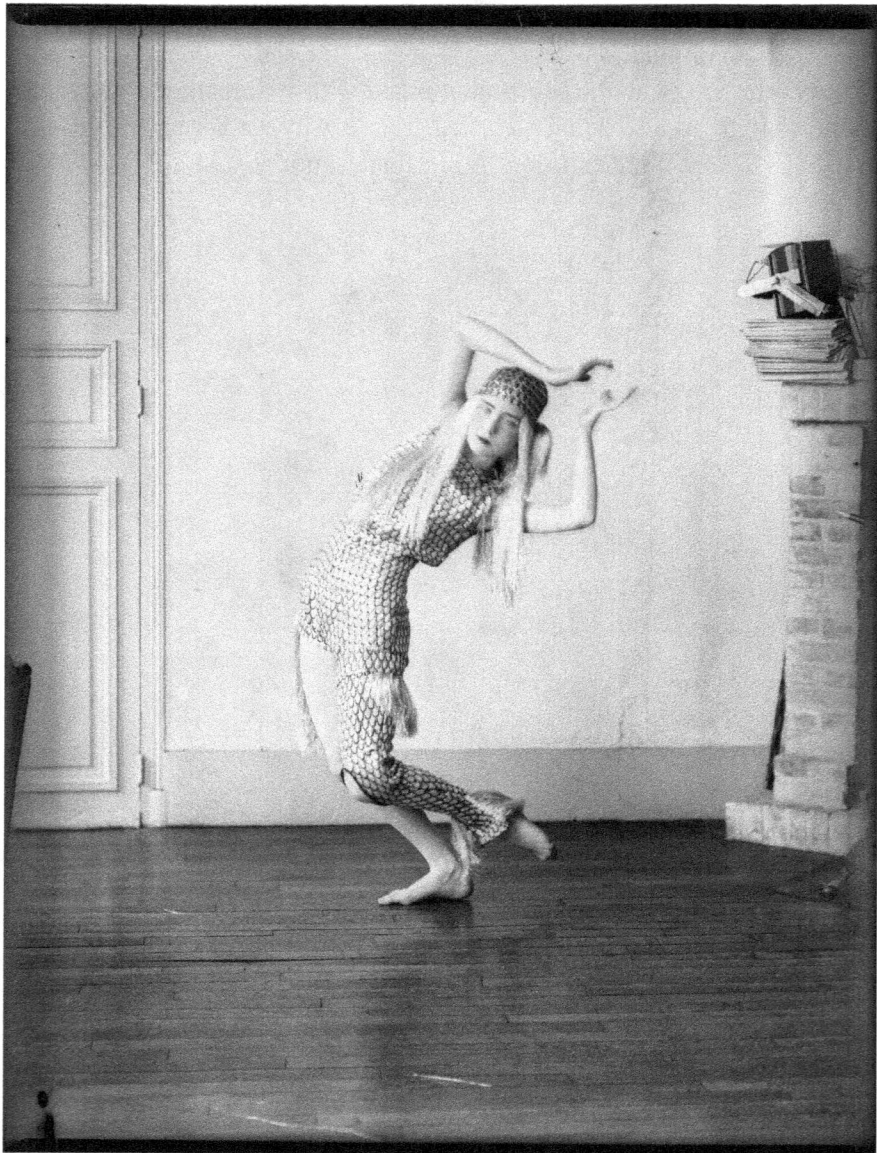

Chapter 9

"But She Talks Just Like I Write"

An often-repeated story describes James Joyce consulting with Carl Jung about his psychotic daughter, Lucia. Joyce was said to have agreed to the consult despite disputing his daughter was seriously ill. He was also openly contemptuous about psychoanalysis—he called Jung "the Swiss Tweedledum who is not to be confused with the Viennese Tweedledee, Dr. Freud."[1] In a letter to his editor and patron, Harriet Shaw Weaver, Joyce described Jung as a man who "amuses himself at the expense (in every sense of the word) of ladies and gentlemen who are troubled with bees in their bonnets."[2]

Jung, so the story goes, said to Joyce, "I'm sorry Mr. Joyce. You want me to tell you that your daughter is really alright, but she is, indeed, a deeply troubled individual." Joyce burst into tears and sobbed, "But she talks just like I write!" "Ah, yes, Mr Joyce," Jung replied, "but you are diving and she is drowning."*

Whether or not the encounter actually transpired this way, one reason the story carries such resonance is that it captures a felt sense that there is a degree of overlap between make-believe, art, genius, and madness, and it is unclear what the relationship between them might be.

Jung's assessment—Joyce dives while Lucia drowns—is commonly understood in terms of "ego structure." Joyce, Jung implies, has sufficient ego structure to channel, and thereby master, the roiling intensities

---

* There is no clear record of the actual conversation between Joyce and Jung. It is known that Jung treated Lucia briefly in psychoanalysis but concluded he couldn't help her. In a private letter, Joyce claimed he had been encouraged to seek help for *himself* ("A batch of people in Zurich persuaded themselves that I was gradually going mad and actually endeavored to induce me to enter a sanatorium," June 21, 1921). Years after the fact, Jung reportedly told Joyce's biographer, Richard Ellman, that Lucia and Joyce were "like two people going to the bottom of a river, one falling and the other diving" (Ellman, p. 692).

DOI: 10.4324/9781003536246-10

of unconscious life. His daughter does not. But what happens if we look at this purported "ego structure" under a higher-powered lens? The psyche has no literal concrete buttresses safeguarding sanity. In fact, it has nothing literal at all.

If we take seriously Winnicott's proposition that imaginative elaboration is what the psyche does, that it is how sensuous experience is structured in thought, then we need to ask: How is it that Joyce could periodically muster imaginative processes to give coherent and shareable shape to the contours of experience, whereas Lucia for the most part could not? To put this metaphorically: When is the imaginative a bridge and when an unfathomable sinkhole? How was it that Joyce reimagined modern literature while his daughter wasted away in a mental asylum? Is it only, as some observers claim, that Joyce was "functional because he was a genius?"[3]

No doubt Joyce was a verbal genius. But what is known of Joyce's personal life—and much is known—suggests he was quite mad in his own way. When he came to Jung, he purportedly described himself as a "man of small virtue, inclined to extravagance and alcoholism."[4] The documented picture is more ruinous. Joyce suffered recurring bouts of nervous fits, lived as an itinerant nomad moving 20 times in the 18 years he resided in Paris, and was frequently forced to flee the ire of unpaid landlords while living lavishly "in the free-spirited way that only the inveterately insolvent can."[5] He wrote to his son that, for half a century, his eyes "gazed into nullity where they have found a lovely nothing."[6] Joyce no doubt meant this both literally—he underwent a series of risky eye surgeries—and figuratively, in regard to his emotional state. Richard Ellman, Joyce's most important biographer, concluded Joyce was "this bizarre and wonderful creature who turned literature and language on end."[7]

Joyce was often remote, arrogant, and aloof. As is common for individuals with a tenuous grasp on their sanity, he could become obsessively focused on certain details of the actual world. One small example offers a window into the mysterious way Joyce managed to transmute arbitrary but actual details into masterful works of fiction: In a pleading letter to his aunt, he is desperate for her to confirm information about a particular existent railing he recalled from his youth in Dublin. Joyce was imagining one of his fictional characters climbing down that railing and he had to know whether it was "possible for an ordinary person to climb over the area railings," have his feet be "within 2 feet or 3 of the ground," and lower himself down safely.[8] It is curious that, while Joyce felt free to invent a fictional being, he could not abide an inaccurate portrayal of the actual railing.

It cannot possibly be that the specificity of the request was solely because Joyce needed his story to be "believable." An author can achieve credibility with far less precision than Joyce demanded regarding a railing in a far-away city. Many authors dispense with accuracy so as to create memorable images. But Joyce seemed to feel that only by confirming his memory could he write something true. His somewhat obsessive focus on this detail suggests a struggle to hold on to something vital. But what is it? While imagining a scene, he cannot find peace until the details align in such a way as to feel authentic—not merely in the literal sense of precision accuracy (Joyce is a novelist, not an engineer!) but in his emotional connection to that distant time and place. By holding on to a detail that affords what Henry James called "palpable intimacy,"[9] Joyce bridges a gap between who he is in the here and now and who he was back there and then. As he imaginatively elaborates a fictional narrative about a railing at 7 Eccles Street in Dublin, he is not evading reality but holding on to it in a way he can make use of. Joyce is returning to the scene of early trauma until its genuineness is felt as real, "but no longer too real, realer than real, or only real."[10]

And here it is worth wondering about the aunt to whom he wrote: Is she merely a vehicle for information or might she also be a source of connection? In writing to her is he imagining *her* seeing the railing just as *he* does? Is her involvement helping him remain grounded?

While writing, Joyce is not merely generating indiscriminate portmanteaus and neologisms as Lucia often did. He is innovating a new literature based on a creative reworking of language. Innovation is not the omnipotence of thought. It is an imaginative refashioning of an established order. Absorbed in the fictional, he maintains a foothold in what is actual. Through the imaginative, he transmutes the contingencies of existence into a narrative "epiphany."[11]

Joyce also sustains imaginative dialogue between what he puts on the page and what comes back to him from the page. This is a far cry from simple projection of unconscious phantasy. Joyce discovers a piece of himself in what he's written, and what he's written—the emerging "art object"—informs his inner experience. Each modifies the other without any need to distinguish between the two. In the realm of the imaginative, static phantasy is not cast onto a blank page, and reality does not constrain or dictate what must be. Instead, an actual world is imbued with personal and shareable meaning.

As Joyce refashions language and experiments with storytelling, an area of overlap is created between how things are and how things could be. A process is set in motion. The imaginative dialogue takes time and often feels painfully "incomplete" or "not quite right." Meanwhile, Joyce also reflects upon what he is doing, looks at his idiosyncratic renderings as if from the outside in. He may have woken up from an absorbed, trance-like or drunken state and found himself surprised or even troubled by the words gathered on the page. But, with luck, after reading them afresh and repeated reworking, he may arrive at a satisfactory rapport, a reciprocal resonance, between who he is and what he has written. Or perhaps not, in which case he tries again. He considers whether it has a place in the actual world, which is to say, potentially shareable with others.

When Joyce claimed Lucia "talks just like I write," he was no doubt correct. She was probably as inventive and intelligent as he was. Some scholars claim she was a vital inspiration to her father, a muse of a sort. Jung called Lucia her father's "*anima inspiratrix*," father and daughter sharing "a kind of mystical identity." "If you know anything of my Anima theory," Jung wrote to Patricia Hutchins, "Joyce and his daughter are a classic example of it."[12] The difference between the two of them, however, is that Lucia was "no genius like her father but merely a victim of her illness." She "cannot help ... talking and thinking in such a way," while Joyce "willed it and moreover developed it with all his creative forces." This, claimed Jung, "explains why he himself did not go over the border."[13]

But is this so? Do genius, will, and creativity *explain* Joyce's relative sanity? Or, might nearly the opposite be true? That for some *inexplicable* reason Joyce retained sufficient imaginative interplay to make forays to and fro over the borders between conscious and unconscious and between perception and hallucination, thereby transforming and making shareable his traumatic experiences? And that Lucia, despite her remarkable talents and force of will, failed to generate imaginative space and instead was entombed in static phantasies and solipsistic unreality? While she was tightly bound to her father, serving as someone else's muse can foreclose finding a genuinely responsive, as opposed to self-serving, other and warp one's relationship with what is actual. Lucia lived in a nightmare. Joyce re-imagined his into a shareable dream.

Born in a pauper's ward, Lucia spent her childhood in squalor, moving from place to place as her father wrote, drank heavily, and lived frivolously.

Nevertheless, she was so naturally endowed that, as she entered adulthood, she showed great promise as a linguist, choreographer, and bohemian experimental dancer. A glowing profile of Lucia in *The Paris Times* in 1928 went so far as to assert that the famous James Joyce "may yet be known as his daughter's father."[14]

At some point, it all fell apart. Why? Nobody knows. Explanations fall short. Lucia was severely hampered as a woman in her time and place. She was devastated to learn she was illegitimate. "If I am a bastard," she reportedly screamed at her mother in one of their rows, "who made me one?"[15] There were unverifiable intimations of incest with her brother. She fell in love with Samuel Beckett, one of her father's literary disciples, who somewhat cruelly told her he was more interested in her father than in her. Beckett later told Peggy Guggenheim he had been cruel; he was "dead and had no feelings; hence he had not been able to fall in love with Lucia." Lucia also had fleeting affairs with her drawing teacher, the American artist Alexander Calder, and a few others, followed by a brief and hopeless engagement to Alec Ponisovsky, a Russian Jew. Lucia's behavior grew increasingly erratic, dramatic, and violent, with her cutting telephone wires, throwing chairs, setting fire to things, and going into a catatonic trance for several days. Joyce forced her to give up dancing as he believed it was taxing her nerves. She was incarcerated against her will in a French sanatorium and diagnosed as schizophrenic. Later, she was taken to the Burghölzli psychiatric clinic in Zurich, where Jung, who was the 20th doctor to see her, concluded her psyche was so bound up with her father's that psychoanalysis could be of no help.

However else one might understand Lucia's troubles, the area of interplay between the imaginative and actual clearly dwindled for her. Whether the waning is a cause or an effect of madness is hard to say. Either way, the outcome is catastrophic. A genius—let alone a "tortured and blocked replica of genius," as Lucia has been described[16]—is not functional just because they are a genius. Prodigious talent and intellect are poor substitutes for a capacity to sustain interplay between the idiosyncratic and consensually validated. They cannot provide psychic equilibrium, allow a person to experience a nightmare as both emotionally real and factually unreal, or bridge the gap between one's traumatic past and the exigencies of making a life. Without an area of interplay, Lucia had no respite from her furtive and ultimately futile search for reciprocal resonance. Unable to find herself outside, she grew vacant inside.

Her father, meanwhile, remained alive in the imaginative realm, achieving through his stories much that was impossible for him in life. He would, as his character Stephen Daedalus said of himself, "create proudly out of the freedom and power of his soul, as the *great artificer* whose name he bore, a living thing, new and soaring and beautiful, impalpable, imperishable."[17] The mythical Daedalus had constructed wings to fly out of imprisonment on Crete. Joyce's Daedalus creates himself anew in the "virgin womb of imagination."[18] However else one might hear this phrase, Joyce's imaginative aliveness—with all its illusion and artifice—gave him leeway, while his daughter, entombed in solipsism, could not create much of a life.

James Joyce remained devoted to Lucia, refusing to acknowledge her madness. Jung believed Joyce's "obstinate reluctance" to accept his daughter's grave illness was because of his own "schizophrenic psychological style."[19] He unconsciously identified with her so much that he could not bear to see the truth. It has been said that Joyce suffered a "gloom of tragic dimensions" in relation to her. Somewhat self-referentially, he also "embraced guilt" over his daughter's misfortune: "Whatever spark of gift I possess has been transmitted to Lucia," he wrote, "and has kindled a fire in her brain."[20]

After James Joyce died suddenly of peritonitis in 1941, Harriet Weaver, his literary patron, had Lucia moved to a secluded mental asylum in England. Lucia's mother never visited. Wasting away there for the rest of her life, she "gazed into the nullity,"[21] finding nothing but void.

Chapter 10

Paracosms in the Parsonage

The Brontë children—Charlotte, Branwell, Emily, and Anne—were born in rapid succession. A mere 20 months after the birth of Anne, their mother died an agonizing death. Four years later, two older siblings died within two weeks of each other, probably from tuberculosis. Patrick Brontë, an eccentric parish priest, was left alone with the four surviving children. After several failed attempts to remarry, including an arrogant offer to a woman he had cruelly jilted years earlier, Patrick removed himself to the remote English countryside, resigning himself to widowerhood. The Brontë children were left to grow up motherless and isolated in a "windswept Parsonage with its unloved patch of thorns abutting graves."[1]

One place the siblings found solace was in their father's library. Books opened up alternative worlds. Soon, they were inventing their own. In 1826, Patrick bought his son, Branwell, 12 wooden soldiers for his ninth birthday. The girls quickly "snatched" some up, claiming them as their own. Calling them the "Young Men" or the "Twelves," the children crafted identities for each soldier, engrossing themselves in creative play.[2]

Gradually, the children emancipated themselves from the concreteness of the physical toys and moved from play-acting to avidly chronicling adventure tales. Charlotte, the oldest, suggested everyone manage an island of their own and name it after a heroic leader. Each sibling became a godlike figure, an omnipotent creator and omniscient narrator of an island built around "the Great Bay at the confluence of rivers in a fictional West Africa."[3] The various islands were united into the "The Glass Town Confederacy," a shared imaginative world. Absorbing material from books in their father's library, local newspapers, and magazines, the children modeled their invented stories on the actual world they read and heard about. The

DOI: 10.4324/9781003536246-11

Brontës became "colonizers—both literally and imaginatively—imitating and reconfiguring the political and social world of 19th century England."[4]

As the adventure stories proliferated and grew ever more elaborate, the children wanted to preserve a record, to keep the memory of the fictional events alive. They rendered the Glass Town chronicles with painstaking precision on folded sheets of paper, 2 inches by 1½ inches in size, stitched together to form miniature books so tiny they could fit in the palms of their hands. The miniaturized books were intended to be small enough for the toy soldiers to read. Perhaps no less salient was that their father had poor eyesight, which meant the micrographic print allowed the children's writing to be kept secret. The chronicles included detailed maps, topographic paintings, sagas of kingdoms steeped in violence, politics, lust, and betrayal. Interspersed were diary-like entries, personal poetry, and prose.

Glass Town's uncensored fictional universe became a central preoccupation of the Brontë siblings well into adulthood. The four siblings wrote both independently and collaboratively, taking great care in the development of storylines and characters. At some point, Charlotte and Branwell developed a new territory called "Angria," an evolution of the Confederacy. Emily and Anne initially contribute to Angria but, in 1831, they "secede" from the Glass Town Confederacy and create a spin-off, which they call "Gondal."

Glass Town, Angria, and Gondal are poignant examples of what are known as paracosms—spontaneously created, highly detailed, and sustained imaginary private worlds—often with their own geography, history, culture, politics, publications, and even language. A paracosm is no fleeting fancy. It is a totally immersive experience originating in childhood and often continuing well into adulthood. Incorporating elements of real-world happenings, invented characters, and a child's perspective on social conventions, a paracosm generates a sophisticated subjective reality with which the creator has a deeply felt and meaningful relationship. Even late in life, childhood paracosms are remembered in remarkable detail, which is why they have been thought of as the "flies in amber of early phantasy life."[5]

Psychiatrists Delmont and Shirley Morrison look at "paracosmic phantasy" from the point of view of unsuccessful childhood grieving. "Imagination," they note, "is the way experience is first represented in childhood thought."[6] In the usual course of development, this "first way of knowing" becomes "more socialized and organized by less egocentric dimensions of thought and more stable, social interpersonal dimensions."[7]

If development is significantly disrupted by catastrophic early loss, the individual can end up a "prisoner of their preoccupation" with the loss.[8] The Morrisons cite examples such as James M. Barrie, the creator of *Peter Pan*, Jack Kerouac, and *Out of Africa* author Isak Dinesen, all of whom suffered early childhood tragedy and developed paracosmic fantasies. Whenever these future authors sat before the blank page to craft a story, conclude the Morrisons, "they did so because they needed to construct a memory to understand loss."[9]

At first glance, the Brontë children fit this pattern as well. The toy soldier dolls that set the paracosm in motion were often buried and reanimated, suggesting a symbolic reversal of death. The very title for their series, "The Glass Town," with its imaginary island of "Angria," gestures to the fragility of their situation and the feelings roiling in what Charlotte called her "world below."[10] It is reasonable to assume, as the Morrisons do, that absorption in the paracosm was to some extent compensatory for the children. Rather than see themselves as motherless, living in poverty, and socially deprived, their paracosm "gave them a sense of being very special, of carrying powers within themselves that far exceeded the ordinary."[11]

However, studies show many eminently creative writers—Anthony Trollope, Robert Louis Stevenson, C.S. Lewis, W.H. Auden among them— as well as highly intelligent McArthur Award recipients with no reported evidence of early trauma, created paracosms in their childhood.[12] It is also true that paracosms are by no means characteristic of most people who suffer similar childhood loss. So, it is worth pondering: What *else* might these intense imaginings be doing for the Brontë children? What can be gleaned from a closer look at the imaginative process involved in creating Gondal and Angria? Is the paracosm only or primarily driven by the disguised need "to construct a memory to understand loss"?

From a psychoanalytic point of view, paracosmic fantasies are frequently interpreted as if they were dreams. Content is examined to identify themes from which unconscious phantasy is inferred. All this is well established. But understanding a paracosm involves more than translation of unconscious phantasy.

Whatever other function it might serve, a paracosm is first and foremost an extended exercise in imaginative curiosity. Driven by curiosity, the Brontë children acquired a tremendous amount of knowledge about the history of the British Empire, which they imaginatively refashioned and integrated into their private parallel world. "The constant adjustment of both the old and the new is imagination," claims the American psychologist and educational reformer John Dewey.[13] "Adjustment" is an active creative process in which the individual reconciles the familiar with the unfamiliar. What matters is not the particular material encountered; it is the process of imaginatively integrating a previously unfamiliar "not-me." Without a personal slant of imaginative curiosity, little real learning occurs.

Imaginative curiosity can run wild. But children who create paracosms diligently systematize their invented world. The English-American poet W.H. Auden created a paracosm—he called it his "private sacred world"— beginning around age six. Auden remarked that in his play he "felt instinctively, without knowing why, that I was bound to obey certain rules."[14]

The same was true of the Brontës. Early on in their play-acting, the children might have haphazardly animated their toy soldiers. But the paracosm as such would not exist were it not for their attaching great importance to preserving its internal consistency. Seemingly far-fetched flights of fancy were organized through a set of consistent assumptions from which they rarely, if ever, deviated. The very idea that the notebooks needed to be small enough for the toy soldiers to read is testimony to that. The events described in the paracosms may, at times, seem improbable, but they are always possible, from the point of view of the terms set forth by the siblings. The paracosms were consistently realistic and naturalistic, in the sense that the stories correspond to real life as the children knew it: Moral dilemmas arise, sins are committed, and there is a fair amount of blood-thirsty warfare.

Yet, even within agreed-upon parameters, there were marked differences among the children regarding which dimensions of experience were given priority. For example, when Branwell and Charlotte created Angria, Branwell was preoccupied with its geography, history, public institutions, and political events. Although Charlotte worked loyally within the terms set forth by Branwell, she threw herself into inventing personal stories about individual characters. The collaborative paracosm obviously held different significance for each child.

Christine Alexander, a Brontë juvenilia historian, describes how Charlotte and Branwell clash as to how best to ensure the consistency of their joint imaginary world. When Branwell exuberantly kills off important characters, Charlotte resurrects them. When Branwell becomes bored with a fictional newsletter, Charlotte steps in and keeps the publication going.[15]

Why must Charlotte rescue characters in what is nothing but make-believe? What makes for the felt "correctness" of how a story must proceed? Clearly, each child has his or her own intense emotional invest-ment: Branwell is disposed to kill off characters; Charlotte needs them to survive. From one point of view, it could be said that each is "projecting" their emotional need onto the characters. But the imaginative process is more subtle than that: Through a recurring back and forth between char-acter and creator, a resonance—a "felt rightness"—is discovered. This res-onance has a consistency all its own, any violation of which is experienced as "off," if not intolerable.

Despite appearing idiosyncratic and even fantastical at times, the Brontës' paracosms also reveal how embedded they all were within what Charles Taylor calls the "social imaginary." Taylor describes the "social imaginary" as "the ways people imagine their social existence, how they *fit together with others* … and the deeper normative notions and images that underlie these expectations."[16]

Every society is constituted through a social imaginary process, a sin-gular way of living in and seeing the world. Castoriadis calls this the "*laces* which tie a society together and the forms which define what, for a given society, is 'real.'"[17] These laces are constituted by a complex set of values, institutions, laws, and symbols through which any given people imagine their collective social life. What appears perfectly "real" to one society might, therefore, feel "unbelievable" to another, at least until the internal logic is apprehended.

We are all inevitably constituted by "social phantasy systems."[18] As Lacan points out, Melanie Klein's work on phantasy, perhaps unwittingly, "pushes back the limits within which we can see the *subjective* function of identification operate."[19] As creatively imaginative as they were, the Brontës' paracosms—with their hierarchies, colonial conquests, and moral codes—were built up from actual elements of the social imaginary world in which they were embedded.

The same is true about imaginary companions, a common precursor of the paracosm. Imaginary companions, who bear many similarities to adult fiction, are part of an important developmental process in which small chil-dren sort out their causal understanding of how human beings relate to each other within a given society. A charming example is Adam Gopnik's three-year-old daughter, in New York City, who created an imaginary companion named "Charlie Ravioli." The little girl walked around the house grumbling about "Mr. Ravioli": He was always too busy, frequently in meetings, and didn't return her phone calls. Occasionally, she would "bump into" Mr.

Ravioli. They would "have coffee" or "grab lunch," but then, inevitably, "he had to run." Gopnik phoned his sister, Alison, a well-known developmental psychologist, asking if he should be concerned about his daughter's preoccupation with Mr. Ravioli. "That sounds *completely* New York!" she responded and hung up the phone. Gopnik eventually realized his daughter's imaginary companion wasn't a marker of trauma. She was giving a name to features of local manners.[20]

The term "imaginary companion" suggests a need for intimate company. But is relief from loneliness the only or even main function they serve? There is absolutely no evidence that children with imaginary companions are lonelier or more socially isolated than their peers. Nor are they necessarily brighter, more creative, withdrawn, or disturbed than other children. The invention of imaginary companions does not necessarily indicate distress or explicit trauma.[21] But they are great examples of psychological counterfactuals, in which every child uses imaginative invention to understand and explore psychological possibilities.[22]

Nevertheless, as is the case with paracosms, there are documented examples pointing in the direction of trauma. When the Mexican painter Frieda Kahlo contracted polio as a child, she created an imaginary companion. Later, as a promising medical student, she was injured in a horrific bus accident, which left her suffering excruciating life-long pain. As an accomplished artist, Kahlo painted her childhood imaginary companion in many of her self-portraits.[23]

The musician Kurt Cobain, who died of a self-inflicted gunshot wound at the age of 27, left behind a suicide note addressed to his childhood imaginary companion, Boddah. According to his biographer, the imaginary companion became a figure of refuge after the dissolution of Cobain's childhood family.[24] Cobain's suicide note to Boddah ends with the passage: "I'm too sensitive. I need to be slightly numb in order to regain the enthusiasms I once had as a child ... It is better to burn out than to fade away."[25]

That Cobain addresses his parting thoughts to an imaginary childhood companion suggests profound isolation from real people in the world. But, more than a wish to die, it expresses Cobain's desperate desire to be alive to burning intensities he recalls from childhood.

Traumatic examples such Kahlo and Cobain, however, may distract from how pervasive the creation of imaginary companions is among children. Their heyday is somewhere between the ages of three and six. This is precisely the developmental period in which children discover fundamental aspects of how minds work, their own and the minds of others. They are developing an understanding of the causal connections between desires and beliefs, emotions and actions. And coming to recognize that different people may believe different things about what is actually true. Marjorie Taylor cites extensive research in cognitive science and child development suggesting children involved with imaginary companions perform notably better on "theory of mind" tasks than children who were not.[26]

Apparently, make-believe companions are a way of making beliefs about what is actual. This is not simply a matter of reality testing. Imaginative elaboration includes active excursions back and forth over the line of what is felt to be real but known to be not real. As such, it is a critical building block in a child's growing capacity to distinguish phantasy from reality while also allowing them to coexist. As self-generated experiments in the interplay between the imaginative and actual, imaginary companions help discover not only the limits of magical thinking (as reality testing suggests) but the power to make what is "not-me" into something of and for oneself.

The shift from an imaginary companion to a paracosm reflects an awareness of an ever-widening and complex social world filled with loyalties, betrayals, alliances, exclusions, heroes, henchmen, and outcasts. In short: A world in which people do things to and with each other. The Brontë children might themselves have been traumatized misfits creating seemingly alternative realities. But, in so doing, they were employing potent imaginative capacities to sort out how triumphs, defeats, passions, and violence actually work in the social world.

And, it can be added, all the while they were keeping an eye on what is actual. The children embed numerous details of their surroundings in the paracosmic text.[27,28] An entry from Emily Brontë, for example, includes a painted sketch of her and her sister at their table writing collaboratively. As she is writing, Emily is painting a picture of herself absorbed in the act of writing. It is as if she is showing herself what she looks like in the altered state of immersion in the paracosm. There are other ways Emily sets the stage, so to speak. Before proceeding with the telling of a story, she relates a detailed account of where each member of the family is at a given moment. One description is of Charlotte in Anne's room writing, while Branwell reads out loud to her and Anne and herself at the dining room table working on the Gondal saga. In another instance, Emily records mundane conversations taking place within the Brontë household such as an aunt appearing to call them to tea. All the while she is absorbed in the imaginary paracosm, Emily busily chronicles actual domestic events without ever losing sight of which is which.

Emily also consciously draws upon and explicitly references actual historical events in moving her fictional plots forward. For example, she writes an elaborate description of an emperor and empress from a city called Gaaldine preparing to depart for Gondal on the 12th of July to participate in a coronation ceremony. Suddenly, she adds: "Queen Victoria ascended the throne this month." It is evident that happenings in the real world weave their way into events in fictional Gondal.

To suggest Emily uses the paracosm only to escape the cruel reality of her situation is to overlook nuances of her experience. The details of everyday life she embeds in the text show her moving in and out of the paracosm. At moments, she enters an imaginatively absorbed state driven by the search for resonant forms for her feelings. Writing is not simply the expression of fully formed thoughts. No less important is the impression the emerging words have upon her. Emily both writes and reads herself, looking to see if it feels "right," or "true" in some hard-to-define, but nevertheless crucial, way. But this singular state of mind must remain uncontested. It will dissolve if the imaginings are judged from the point of view of a distinction between "real" and "not real," or if she is forced to attend to what is outside the world she is creating.

But Emily also takes care to return herself to another state of mind in which she holds on to what is actual, tracks it, makes sure it remains in place. Some pieces of actual material may be brought in, imaginatively elaborated, and woven into the fabric of the text. But others will simply be noticed and offer reassurance that, despite the felt reality of the paracosm, the world "out there" remains standing. Exercising a degree of control over transitions between these states of mind allows Emily to risk entering the paracosm without dread of getting so lost in it as to never find her way out.[29] By virtue of trust in her capacity to *both enter and exit* states of imaginative absorption, Emily uses writing not only as an escape from pain but as an opportunity to imaginatively elaborate pain and as a pleasure in its own right.

The same is true for Charlotte, even after she departs home to take up a teaching position at Roe Head, a school in West Yorkshire. Charlotte was quite unhappy at Roe Head and clearly longed to escape from her duties back into an imaginative space. Her continued use of micrographic lettering harkens back to her earlier collaboration with her siblings and suggests continuity with her self as a child. Charlotte's writings at Roe Head include moments when, like her sister Emily, she shuttles between realities. Once, she is writing a sexually charged scene set in Africa. She records someone suddenly knocking on the door and bringing in a plate of butter. At another moment, a pupil suddenly "jolts her back to reality" while she is immersed in Angria.[30] These disruptions could be quite jarring. Creative imaginings require a protected space. For the writer, the sudden cessation of writing can be like coitus interruptus. Charlotte is acquiring experience in living through the inherent strain of having one reality impinge upon another.

Ann Dinsdale, principal curator at the Brontë Parsonage Museum, describes the paracosmic notebooks as "a weird mix of fact and phantasy."[31] From a psychoanalytic point of view, it might be more accurate to say they are a curious amalgam of unconscious phantasy, dissociative daydreaming, the actual, and the imaginative. To the extent that certain themes recur rather than evolve, they can likely be traced back to static phantasy. An example of this might be Charlotte's penchant for resurrecting dead characters. By their own accounts, the children were reclusive and engaged in a fair amount of dissociative daydreaming. As Charlotte once remarked, whenever her favorite characters appeared in the midst of her drab surroundings, she suddenly felt "quite gone."[32] Employed to escape from and compensate for a difficult-to-bear reality, this kind of "phantasying" impedes psychic movement. As Winnicott points out, "In the phantasying, what happens happens immediately, except that it does not happen at all."[33]

At the same time, however, there is also a highly imaginative element evident in the paracosms. Unlike phantasying, imaginative activity is not an intermission from real life; it does not aim to stop time and guarantee nothing actually happens either within the person or between people. Rather than substitute for reality, the imaginative makes responsive use of the actual. It promotes psychic movement—the enhancement of our capacity to think, feel, and generate meaning—rousing experience from the deadness of the concrete. Imagining is the spontaneous continuation of dream life into waking life. Dream life imaginatively weaves its way into living in the real world, and living in the real world weaves its way into dreaming. Imagining allows a person to reach further toward who they might yet become.

Early on, Charlotte already imagined herself a published author. At age 14, she produced a volume of poetry entitled *THE POETASTER*, a neologism both presaging Wallace Stevens's description of poetry as "tasting at the root of the tongue the unreal of what is real"[34] and suggestive of the synesthetic dimension of the imaginative. Charlotte carefully crafted a cover for her volume including the words: "Published By No One/Possessed by EveryOne/Sold by all other booksellers."[35] Years later, when she actually publishes her work, she does so under a male pseudonym. While Charlotte was clearly hampered by and railed against the oppressive constraints society placed on women, it is also true her long experience adopting the perspective of male characters accustomed her to experiencing the world from the points of view of alternative identities. In retrospect, one can see that, well before becoming a published author, Charlotte used the paracosm to refine her craft as a writer. The imaginative play of childhood became a literary workshop, a self-invented apprenticeship including experimentation with genres and cultivation of sensibility. The Brontës may not have published much in their short lifetimes but, by the time they were ready to do so, they were adept handlers of literary forces, knowing "how best to speak to all that excitement and passion and at the same time make it disciplined and realistic, too."[36]

It is also true, however, that, even as the Brontë siblings displayed remarkable creativity, each one struggled mightily to cope imaginatively with the world beyond the paracosm. Brontë researchers have meticulously documented every indication of their emotional instability.[37,38] None of the siblings managed to establish a truly congenial footing outside the parsonage. The Brontë researcher Margaret Lane concluded the siblings "craved their dream world" as if it were a drug, engaging in a "profound turning away from, or refusal of, ordinary life."[39]

Even during their short lifetimes, acquaintances warned about stoking flames of immersive daydreams. At one point, Charlotte sent a sample of her work to the poet Robert Southey, asking his opinion. Southey implored her to step back from the abyss of the "visionary world" in which she "habitually indulged." Daydreams such as hers, he cautioned, "are likely to induce a distempered state of mind, & in proportion as all the 'ordinary uses the world' seem to you 'flat & unprofitable,' you will be unfitted for them, without becoming fitted for anything else."[40]

Emily seemed even less equipped than Charlotte. Taciturn by nature, she frequently ran off to the moors to avoid other people. When forced against her will to join Charlotte at Roe Head School on the eve of her 17th birthday, Emily fell depressively ill. During the three-month ordeal, Charlotte feared for her life. Only once ensconced back in the parsonage and immersed again in her poetry and private paracosm did Emily regain strength. While failing to thrive in the wider world, she cultivates a rather frenzied fantasied fusion with a creative spirit she calls her "Visitant." Blending elements of devout, visionary, and heretical Christianity, Emily's poems vividly portray her seduction of the "Visitant" and herself as the object of its romantic love.[41]

Emily became a "mystic of the moors."[42] To put this in the language of psychoanalysis: She was swept up in an idealized relationship with what Charles Rycroft calls a "hallucinatory imago."[43] Feverish phantasying about the "Visitant" no doubt felt intensely exciting. But it could not promote emotional growth because there was too little interplay between the imaginative and actual. In the absence of communication with external reality, Emily was stranded in solipsistic unreality, feeding only off herself.

Falling in love is an imaginative act. It requires a bringing together or convergence of an actual external object with a "hallucinated" internal one. In Emily's short life, there was never such imaginative alignment, no vitalizing interplay between what she conjured and what she found outside herself. There was only dissociated phantasying in which desire and reality remained inevitably and achingly in opposition. As phantasying triumphed over imagining for Emily, no spark of adult erotic connection with an actual available other could be kindled.

Emily did, however, harbor passionate feelings toward her siblings, particularly Anne and Branwell. According to Ellen Nussey, Charlotte's lifelong friend and frequent visitor at the parsonage, Emily and Anne were "like twins," "inseparable companions," and "in the very closest sympathy which never had any interruption."[44] And Emily fell deathly ill immediately following Branwell's funeral. When she died less than three months later, their housemaid remarked that "Miss Emily died of a broken heart for love of her brother."[45]

Branwell, too, reminds us that being highly imaginative is no guarantee of a better life; his was a "downhill race toward self-destruction."[46] A year younger than Charlotte, Branwell was remarkably intelligent and often the leader in the play-acting and prolific paracosms. He had a prodigious grasp of facts, "documenting in encyclopedic detail in neat lists, footnotes, sketches and maps, the geography, history, government, and social structure of the Glass Town Federation" and, later, Angria.[47] There was much rivalry between him and his sisters, particularly Charlotte. He despised Charlotte's "frivolity" and "foolish romances," which, he said, encroached upon the "somberness" and "gravity" of his sagas.[48] Over time, Charlotte voiced concern about her brother's "almost insane devotion to all the celebrated characters."[49] It disturbed her to see him impersonating his own characters.

One sees in Charlotte's early concerns the seeds of Branwell's eventual ruin. As he grew older, there were uncomfortable situations in which Branwell boastfully exaggerated, as some of the rogue characters did in his fictional accounts. He adopts the bombastic swagger of one of his invented characters in unsolicited letters to Wordsworth and a literary editor. Put off by his tone, they do not respond. To be clear: It is not that Branwell was *delusional* about the "reality" of the paracosm. Like his sisters, Branwell was fully aware his paracosm was fictional. But the line blurred between his personhood and his fictional creations. That Branwell became a caricature of his own characters suggests dissociative fragility, a fragmented and unstable sense of himself. Descending into drink, opium addiction, financial profligacy, and sexual indiscretions, Branwell eventually garners a reputation as "a specter in the Brontë story, in pathetic contrast with the astonishing achievements of his sisters."[50]

It has been suggested that, in response to long-term trauma, certain children create "post-traumatic paracosms,"[51] and that developmental problems emerge from over-involvement in a world only of one's own. The year his mother died, Branwell, then age eight, swore he heard her crying outside in the cold, begging to be let back in.[52] A Brontë biographer suggests Branwell was re-traumatized by the sudden death of his eldest sister, Maria, who had been a "little mother" to him following the loss of his birth mother and by the expectations placed upon him as an only boy.[53]

Branwell was a fairly accomplished painter. A disturbing portrait he paints at age 17 shows vibrant likenesses of his three sisters with his own figure literally effaced, blotted out. As the ghostly blur covering his visage suggests, his physical body might be present but his spirit is elsewhere. It was not that Branwell was unable to discern reality; it was that his psyche and soma seemed not of a piece. Branwell's difficulties feeling alive and real *as himself* are a failure more of personalization than of reality testing per se. It is no wonder that, when faced with the challenges of ordinary life, Branwell retreats into a dissociative, hazy irreality, both self- and drug-induced.

For Branwell, the paracosm was probably the one area of imaginative creation in which he could feel intensely alive. In moments of distress, he turned to the paracosm as Cobain did to his imaginary friend, Boddah. Through his relationship to the paracosm, Branwell generated resonant images that made it possible to briefly bear both the stark immediacy and transience of things. But, for Branwell, even when the paracosm worked, it was too split off from his experience of himself as a person in the actual world. And, at some point, it, too, no longer worked. Branwell was left with only pain, the consequences of numbing the pain, and his irreal relations with external reality.

"In the end," claims Winnicott, "the self is not really to be found in what is made out of products of body or mind."[54] Although an artistic creation might be valuable in terms of skill or beauty, it "never heals the underlying lack of sense of self."[55] Nor does a paracosm, as pleasurable as it may be, make up for missing resonant responses of significant others. Like his sister Emily, Branwell was enormously creative but failed to invest his prodigious imaginative capacities to live creatively in the actual world of people. Displaying much frenetic activity but little genuine vitality, he ended up an "as if" version of himself.

All four Brontë siblings died young. Charlotte, who lived the longest, was dead by age 39. Whatever else one might think about their intense absorption in the paracosm, there can be no doubt it carried tremendous personal significance for each of them. "What a privilege is reverie." wrote Charlotte later in life. "I am thankful. I have the power of solacing myself with the dream of creations, whose reality I shall never behold."[56]

The paracosm was Charlotte's primary vehicle for transitional relatedness—the unique experience of an object, animate or inanimate, as a source of *solace*. Solace is a sometimes-disparaged term in psychoanalysis. But the consolations of transitional relatedness are vital to bearing the inherent strain of being alive and the fact of one's essential aloneness. Charlotte drew upon "the power of solacing" not only as antidote to early misfortunes but to weather ongoing difficulties in living. The problem was not that she used the paracosm in this way. It was that she found too little solace born of transitional relatedness anywhere else. Transitional relating—what she calls her "dream of creations"—was accessible *only* in relation to "a reality" she "shall never behold."

Charlotte Brontë related to the paracosm as she did to the art of fiction itself: She knew it to be make-believe but insisted it really mattered! We are, nevertheless, left with difficult-to-reconcile impressions: From one point of view, the Brontës' paracosms express a natural desire for intense imaginative experience and constitute a highly valuable form of transitional relatedness. From another, they become a somewhat mad withdrawal from the actual world. Perhaps it is best to leave the last word to Charlotte her-self: "When authors write best," she once remarked, "an influence seems to waken in them which becomes their master, which will have its own way, putting out of view, all behests, but its own." And Charlotte poses a question faced daily in psychoanalytic practice: "Should we try to coun-teract this influence? Can we indeed counteract it?"[57]

Coda

If you have stayed with this book until now, you no doubt noted the liberty I have taken in elaborating Winnicott's view of the psyche as an ongoing source of imaginative elaboration. The imaginative—at least how I employ the term—is not mere mental imagery, a mistress of error and duplicity, or the opposite of what is real. Imagining, a present continuous verb, entails a primal play of psyche-soma in relation to the possibility of things. It idiosyncratically imbues experience with a sense of aliveness, richness, and intelligibility by transforming impressions into perceptions and unconscious stirrings into fathomable thoughts. Wayward and refractory, the imaginative carries the potential to promote psychic movement, to enhance one's capacity to feel, think, and generate meaning, rousing experience from the deadness of the concrete.

Imagining gestures toward a view of aliveness as something distinct from either sexuality or self-preservation. The world feels one way when we are alive to it and quite another when we are not. Intimately bound up with the question of what authentically makes experience feel personal, the imaginative, I think it fair to say, makes us more fully human.

Even as we are embedded in what is, imagining allows leeway to weave ourselves into what might yet be. But leeway is not free reign. It is a mistake to conflate the imaginative with the good, for the imaginative is no guarantor of a better life. Alongside imaginative investment in experience there is, in health, also a hunger for truth, a need to know what is actual and to demystify falsehoods masquerading as truth. That is why it makes a world of difference how one navigates the inherently precarious interplay between the imaginative and actual. The imaginative, after all, can just as easily veer from the veridical as it can serve as a life-enhancing bridge to apprehending and even altering what is actual.

DOI: 10.4324/9781003536246-12

Many difficulties in living result from breakdowns in the interplay between the imaginative and actual. I've suggested names—abject reality, solipsistic unreality, dissociative irreality, and degrees of denialism—to describe the potentially profound consequences of such breakdowns. A capacity to enliven reality while seeing things for what they are can never be taken for granted.

The poet Elizabeth Bishop's grandmother had a glass eye. The glass eye often looked heavenward, or off at an angle, while the real eye looked directly at you. Bishop was so fascinated by this that, over the years, she repeatedly reworked a poem about it. Her grandmother's gaze struck Bishop as rather like the situation of the poet: "[T]he difficulty of combining the real with the decidedly un-real ... the curious effect a poem produces of being as normal as sight and yet as synthetic, as artificial, as a glass eye."[1]

Bishop's grandmother's bifurcated gaze is also a useful metaphor for the inherent difficulty involved in reconciling the imaginative and the actual, distinct from what psychoanalysis commonly describes as conflict between reality and pleasure. Freud's principles of mental functioning needn't be reduced to only two. The imaginative generates an inherent strain of keeping inner and outer separate while, at the same time, maintaining interplay between them. We don't simply see an objective reality or solely invent a subjective one. Development is not the triumph of the former over the latter.

"Kodochrome,"[2] a popular song written by Paul Simon, was inspired by childhood memories of vibrant images his father, an amateur photographer, captured when color film was first introduced. Seeing prints awash in vibrant colors made photographs come alive. Everything, Simon realized, looks so much worse in black and white.

"Kodachrome" is often heard as a requiem for the passing of time, an expression of nostalgia and fondness for the intensities of childhood. But the song, as I hear it, also suggests a deeper communication: Simon craves an experience of aliveness that has roots in, but is not confined to, childhood. Even as the adult in him acknowledges reality never quite matches his fervent imaginings, Simon nevertheless pleads desperately, to his mother of all people, not to take his Kodachrome away. He dreads what life might feel like without it. He craves the vibrancy, not of any Kodachrome, but of *his* Kodachrome. And, in turning to his mother, he intuits how the pulse of life is bound up in early illusory experiences with her.

Retaining a connection to these early experiences, Simon creatively transforms a childhood memory into song. He might not feel good while composing, creative work can be quite painful. But, with luck and persistence, something eventually comes to feel alive and real and true for Simon. He has an intimate experience as he refines the truth he can tell himself and share with others. For a moment, the landscape shimmers.

The word illusion, which in various guises has been a thread in this volume, needs to be shaken loose from its connotation as merely misguided tricks our minds play upon us. Developmentally, illusion precedes the distinction between fact and fantasy, and it remains a primary area of experiencing in which we are released from the need to differentiate between inner and outer. Illusion is not a mixing, overlapping, or some combination of fact and phantasy. It is *a singular uncontested state of mind*, which is a source of vitality throughout life. Asking the question "Is it real or not real?" immediately explodes the experience itself.

The writer Margaret Atwood describes how every author has something akin to a double, the one who writes but is all too often mistakenly conflated with the person of the writer. She wonders about the peculiar state of mind entailed in the actual writing.

Atwood finds an analogy in Lewis Carroll's *Alice through the Looking-Glass*: At the outset of the tale, Alice is on the life side of the mirror, while another Alice, her reflection and double, is on the art side. Each looks at the other, as if from afar. But, rather than break the mirror, abandon art, and inhabit "the hard and bright 'life' side, where the 'art' side is doomed to die," Alice goes *through* the mirror. The "real" Alice merges with the "imagined Alice, the dream Alice, the Alice who exists nowhere." And, when the "real Alice" returns to the waking world, she tells the story of that other world to her cat.

"The act of writing," says Atwood,

takes place at the moment when Alice passes through the mirror. At this one instance, the glass barrier between the doubles dissolves, and Alice is neither here nor there, neither art nor life, neither the one thing, nor the other, though at the same time she is all of these at once. At that moment, time itself stops, and also stretches out, and both writer and reader have all the time not in the world.[3]

Atwood reminds us that writing emerges only when "the double dissolves," and a singular state of interplay between the imaginative and actual is allowed for and tolerated.

The Israeli poet Lea Goldberg, however, reminds us that Atwood's doubles do not necessarily live in harmony with each other. The person emerging from the uncontested illusory state might very well be acutely aware of the precarious relationship between their physical being and poetic self. A brief fragment in one of Goldberg's final journal entries, written as she lay dying, reads:

> The distance between me and the poem's she
> Is like the distance between my body and its shadow
> On the wall. But I'll die, she'll remain
> And today I cannot forgive her that.[4]

Goldberg gives voice to a fraught awareness that the liberty and leeway of psyche-soma operates in a realm beyond the concreteness of her actual failing physical body. In the end, she was right: The poet Lea Goldberg outlived Lea Goldberg.

Taken together, the diverse images presented in this book suggest the vestiges of our earliest experiences of betweenness—between mother and infant, between the compliant and the spontaneous, between the imitative and the creative, between what is and what might be—become the rudiments of our later well-being. They lay down a legacy of interplay with which we pass through the mirror between life and art.

It is often claimed that psychoanalysis aims to help a person make sense of their life. But it is worth considering what making sense even means, especially when looked at through a high-powered lens. Making sense is not an exercise in getting disparate pieces of one's self in fixed alignment. Life may be puzzling, but it is not a puzzle to be solved.

While the mind may organize, categorize, catalogue, and collate, it is the psyche's imaginative elaboration that allows experiences to feel meaningful.[5] Without the work of the imaginative, nothing would be fathomable, let alone believable. As the Irish poet Yeats proclaimed, in language simple and direct:

God guard me from those thoughts men think
In the mind alone;
He that sings a lasting song
Thinks in a marrow-bone.[6]

Yeats reminds us that creative living does not arise from a split-off mind. It entails the work of the imaginative in relation to what the world has to offer. That is why psychoanalysis may have little to do with making sense in terms of understanding. But psychoanalysis potentially does provide a setting and a relationship in which, among other things, one may be in touch with both the folly and passion of one's imaginative depth, find a way to be on better terms with the inherent strain between the imaginative and actual, and live with the unpredictability of what makes one's personal landscape shimmer.

It is fitting to give the final word to an image conjured by Mary Oliver:

Whoever you are, no matter how lonely,
the world offers itself to your imagination,
calls to you like the wild geese, harsh and exciting—
over and over announcing your place
in the family of things.[7]

Chapter Notes

Introduction: A Shimmering Landscape

1. Raymond Foye interview with James Schuyler: https://raymondfoye.info/2019/03/18/interview-with-james-schuyler/, italics added.
2. Stevens, W. (1990). "Holiday in Reality." In *The Collected Poems of Wallace Stevens*. U.S. Vintage reissue edition, p. 313.
3. Wood, J. (2015). *The Nearest Thing to Life*. Brandeis University Press, p. 38.
4. Wordsworth, W. (1798). "Essay on Morals." In *The Prose Works of William Wordsworth*, ed. W.J.B. Owen and J.W. Smyser. London: Oxford University Press, 1974, p. 103.
5. Winnicott, D.W. (1971). *Playing and Reality*. Tavistock Publications, p. 3.
6. Taylor, C. (2004). *Modern Social Imaginaries*. Duke University Press.
7. Segal, H. (1957). Notes on Symbol Formation. *International Journal of Psychoanalysis* 38: 391–7.
8. Winnicott, D.W. (1986). *Home Is Where We Start From: Essays by a Psychoanalyst*, ed. C. Winnicott, R. Shepherd, and M. Davis. New York: W.W. Norton, p. 40.
9. Winnicott, D.W. (1971). "Creativity and Its Origins." In *Playing and Reality*. Tavistock Publications, p. 80.
10. O'Connor, F. (1988). *The Habit of Being: Letters of Flannery O'Connor*. New York: Farrar, Straus & Giroux, p. 100.
11. Winnicott, D.W. (1949). "Mind and Its Relation to the Psyche-Soma." In *Through Paediatrics to Psycho-Analysis*. New York: Basic Books, 1975, pp. 243–54, p. 244.
12. Freud, S. (1911). "Formulations on the Two Principles of Mental Functioning." In *The Standard Edition of the Complete Psychological Works of Sigmund Freud*, XII: 213–26.
13. Shepard, O. (ed.). (1961). *The Heart of Thoreau's Journals*. New York: Dover Publications, p. 212.
14. Woolf, V. (1928). *Orlando: A Biography*. Kindle version, Chapter 4, p. 88.
15. Tedeschi, J., and Tedeschi, A. (1990). "Clues: Roots of an Evidential Paradigm." In *Myths, Emblems, and the Historical Method*. Baltimore: Johns Hopkins University Press, p. 102.
16. Milner, M. (1952). Aspects of Symbolism in Comprehension of the Not-Self. *International Journal of Psychoanalysis* 33: 181–94, p. 186.
17. Tennyson, A. (1850). "In Memoriam A.H.H.," Canto XLIV, www.online-literature.com/tennyson/718/
18. Ehrenzweig, A. (1971). *The Hidden Order of Art*. Berkeley and Los Angeles: University of California Press.
19. Winnicott, D.W. (1971). "Creativity and Its Origins." In *Playing and Reality*. Tavistock Publications, p. 70.
20. Barron, S., Draguet, M., and Tashjiian, D. (2006). *Magritte and Contemporary Art: The Treachery of Images*. Ludion/Los Angeles County Museum of Art.

21. Winnicott, D.W. (1969). The Use of an Object. *International Journal of Psychoanalysis* 50: 711–6.
22. Eliot, G. (1990). "The Natural History of German Life." In George Eliot, *Selected Essays, Poems, and Other Writings*. London: Penguin Classic, p. 110.
23. MacIntyre, A. (1981). *After Virtue: A Study in Moral Theory*. University of Notre Dame Press. First edition (January 1, 1981), p. 216
24. Wood, J. (2015). *The Nearest Thing to Life*. Brandeis University Press.
25. Ellmann, R. (1982). *James Joyce*. London: Oxford University Press, p. 692.
26. Bion, W.R. (1963). *Elements of Psycho-Analysis*. Psychoanalytic Electronic Publishing version. 4: 98–104, p. 103.

Chapter 1 "Life Is a Dream. 'Tis Waking That Kills Us"

1. Woolf, V. (1928). *Orlando: A Biography*. Kindle version, Chapter 4, p. 88.
2. Wilbur, R. (2004). "At Moorditch." In *Richard Wilbur: Collected Poems 1943–2004.*   New York: Harcourt, p. 32.
3. Freud, S. (1911). "Formulations on the Two Principles of Mental Functioning." In *The Standard Edition of the Complete Psychological Works of Sigmund Freud*, XII: 213–26.
4. Freud, S. (1923). "The Ego and the Id." In *The Standard Edition of the Complete Psychological Works of Sigmund Freud*, XIX: 17, italics added.
5. Freud, S. (1911). "Formulations on the Two Principles of Mental Functioning." In *The Standard Edition of the Complete Psychological Works of Sigmund Freud*, XII: 221.
6. Freud, S. (1933). "New Introductory Lectures on Psycho-Analysis." In *The Standard Edition of the Complete Psychological Works of Sigmund Freud*, XXII: 79.
7. Freud, S. (1897). "Letters to Fliess." In *The Standard Edition of the Complete Psychological Works of Sigmund Freud*, I: 247, italics added.
8. Freud, S. (1892). [Notes I] from Extract from the Fliess Papers. In *The Standard Edition of the Complete Psychological Works of Sigmund Freud*, I: 248–50.
9. Freud, S. (1897). "Letters to Fliess." In *The Standard Edition of the Complete Psychological Works of Sigmund* Freud, I: 247.
10. Freud, S. (1906). "Creative Writers and Day Dreaming." In *The Standard Edition of the Complete Psychological Works of Sigmund Freud*, IX: 145–6.
11. Freud, S. (1917). "Introductory Lectures on Psycho-Analysis, Part III, General Theory of the Neuroses." In *The Standard Edition of the Complete Psychological Works of Sigmund Freud*, XVI: 371–2.
12. Freud, S. (1917). "Introductory Lectures on Psycho-Analysis, Part III, General Theory of the Neuroses." In *The Standard Edition of the Complete Psychological Works of Sigmund Freud*, XVI: 371.
13. Freud, S. (1906). "Creative Writers and Day Dreaming." In *The Standard Edition of the Complete Psychological Works of Sigmund Freud*, IX: 144.
14. Winnicott, D.W. (1949). "Mind and Its Relation to the Psyche-Soma." In *Through Paediatrics to Psycho-Analysis*. New York: Basic Books, 1975, pp. 243–54, p. 244, italics in original.
15. Winnicott, D.W. (1956). "Primary Maternal Preoccupation." In *Through Paediatrics to Psycho-Analysis*. New York: Basic Books, 1975, pp. 300–5, p. 303.
16. Harris, P. (2000). *The Work of Imagination: Understanding Children's Worlds*. Oxford: Blackwell.
17. Le Guin, U. (2011). "It Doesn't Have to Be the Way It Is." In *No Time to Spare: Thinking About What Matters*. Boston and New York: Houghton Mifflin Harcourt, 2017, p. 80, italics in original.
18. Winnicott, D.W. (1971). *Playing and Reality*. Tavistock Publications, p. 3.

19. Rodman, F. (2003). *Winnicott: Life and Work*. New York: Perseus Books, p. 373
20. Karen Melikian, personal communication. December 3, 2023.
21. Rycroft, C. (1968). *Imagination and Reality*. New York: International Universities Press, p. 106.
22. Winnicott, D.W. (1969a). "The Pill and the Moon." In *Home Is Where We Start From: Essays by a Psychoanalyst*, ed. C. Winnicott, R. Shepherd, and M. Davis. New York: W.W. Norton, 1986, pp. 195–209, pp. 208–9.
23. Goldman, D. (1993). *In Search of the Real: The Origins and Originality of D.W. Winnicott*. Northvale, NJ: Jason Aronson.
24. Baudry, F. (2009). Winnicott's 1968 Visit to the New York Psychoanalytic Society and Institute: A Contextual View. *Psychoanalytic Quarterly* 78: 1059–90.
25. Rycroft, C. (1968). *Imagination and Reality*. New York: International Universities Press, p. 33
26. Laplanche, J. and Ponytails, J.B. (1973). *The Language of Psycho-Analysis*. New York: W.W. Norton, pp. 314–5.
27. Cited in Castoriadis, C. (1997). *World in Fragments: Writings on Politics, Society, Psychoanalysis, and Imagination*. Stanford University Press, p. 216.
28. Bion, W.R. (1967). A Theory of Thinking. In *Selected Papers on Psycho-Analysis*. New York: Jason Aronson. p. 111.
29. Bion, W. (1962). *Learning from Experience*. Lanham, MD: Rowman & Littlefield, p. 7.
30. Poe, E.A. (1848). *The Complete Tales and Poems of Edgar Allan Poe*. New York: Barnes & Noble, 1992, p. 80.
31. Santayana, G. (1989). *Interpretations of Poetry and Religion*. Cambridge, MA: MIT Press, p. 156.
32. Stern, D.B. (2003). *Unformulated Experience: From Dissociation to Imagination in Psychoanalysis*. London and New York: Routledge.
33. Stern, D.B. (2023). The Person Who Sees the Ship: Language, Imagination, and Being in Unformulated Experience. Talk given at the Westchester Center for the Study of Psychoanalysis and Psychotherapy (WCSPP), November 18, 2023.
34. Stern, D.B. (2023). The Person Who Sees the Ship: Language, Imagination, and Being in Unformulated Experience. Talk given at the Westchester Center for the Study of Psychoanalysis and Psychotherapy (WCSPP), November 18, 2023.
35. Winnicott, D.W. (1986). *Home Is Where We Start From: Essays by a Psychoanalyst*, ed. C. Winnicott, R. Shepherd, and M. Davis. New York: Norton. pp. 49–52.
36. Winnicott, D.W. (1965). "New Light on Children's Thinking." In *Psychoanalytic Explorations*. Cambridge, MA: Harvard University Press, pp. 152–7, p. 157.
37. Santayana, G. (2011). *The Life of Reason, Introduction and Reason in Common Sense*. Cambridge, MA: MIT Press, p. 32.
38. Wordsworth, W. (1805). "The Prelude." In *William Wordsworth: The Major Works*, ed. S. Gill. New York: Oxford University Press, 2008, p. 399.
39. Barth, J.R. (1977). *The Symbolic Imagination: Coleridge and the Romantic Tradition*. Princeton, NJ: Princeton University Press, p. 83.
40. Richards, I.A. (1969). *Coleridge on Imagination*. Bloomington, IN: Indiana University Press, p. 57.
41. Kandel, E. (2012). *Age of Insight: The Quest to Understand the Unconscious in Art, Mind, and Brain*. New York: Random House, p. 202.
42. Wordsworth, W. (1996). *The Prelude*. Penguin Classics. Revised edition, p. 240.
43. Frith, C. (2007). *Making Up the Mind: How the Brain Creates Our Mental World*. Malden, MA: Blackwell Publishing, p. 132.
44. Bell, D. (2016). "The World as It Is vs the World as I Would Like It to Be." In *On Freud's "Formulations of Two Principles of Mental Functioning,"* ed. G. Legaretta and L. Brown. London and New York: Routledge, pp. 39–64.

45. Freud, S. (1913). "Totem and Taboo: Some points of Agreement Between the Mental Lives of Savages and Neurotics." In *The Standard Edition of the Complete Psychological Works of Sigmund Freud*, XIII: 86.
46. O'Connor, F. (1988). *The Habit of Being: Letters of Flannery O'Connor.* New York: Farrar, Straus & Giroux, p. 100.
47. Segal, H. (1957). Notes on Symbol Formation. *International Journal of Psychoanalysis* 38: 391–7.
48. Winnicott, D.W. (1971). "Creativity and Its Origins." In *Playing and Reality*. Tavistock Publications, p. 71.
49. Bell, D. (2016). "The World as It Is vs the World as I Would Like It to Be." In *On Freud's "Formulations of Two Principles of Mental Functioning,"* ed. G. Legaretta and L. Brown. London and New York: Routledge, p. 53–4.
50. Brodsky, J. (1979). "Less Than One." *New York Review of Books*, September 27, 1979.
51. Quoted in Zalewski, D. (2009). "The Background Hum, Ian McEwan's Art of Unease." *The New Yorker*, February 23, 2009.
52. Bach, S. (1985). *Narcissistic States and the Therapeutic Process.* New York: Jason Aronson, p. 23.
53. Sodre, I. (1998). "Death by Daydreaming." In *Psychoanalysis and Culture: A Kleinian perspective*, ed. D. Bell. Tavistock/Duckworth: Tavistock Clinic Series, 1998.
54. Shakespeare, W. (1969). *A Midsummer Night's Dream.* In *The Complete Pelican Shakespeare*. London: Penguin, p. 169.
55. Marion Milner quoted in Caldwell, L. (2000). *Art, Creativity and Living.* London: Karnac, p. 144.
56. Fassin, D. (2007). *When Bodies Remember: Experiences and Politics of AIDS in South Africa.* University of California Press, p. 115.
57. DiResta, R. (2019). "Mediating Consent." Ribbonfarm: Constructions in Magical Thinking. www.ribbonfarm.com/2019/12/17/mediating-consent/
58. Lifton, R.J. (2019). *Losing Reality: On Cults, Cultism, and the Mindset of Political and Religious Zealotry.* New York and London: The New Press. Kindle edition.
59. Blackmur, R.P. (1935). Statements and Idyls, a Review of Norman Macleod's, 'Horizons of Death,' *Poetry* XLVI, May 1935, p. 108.

Chapter 2 Lion-Man

1. Cook, J. (2017) *The Lion Man: An Ice Age Masterpiece.* www.britishmuseum.org/blog/lion-man-ice-age-masterpiece
2. MacGregor, N. (2017, October 23). "Living with the Gods.". BBC Radio 4 Series, *The Beginnings of Belief.* Retrieved April 9, 2023. www.bbc.co.uk/sounds/play/b099xhmj
3. Langer, S. (1942). *Philosophy in a New Key.* Cambridge, MA: Harvard University Press, p. 51.
4. Freud, S. (1913 [1912–1913]). "Totem and Taboo: Some points of Agreement Between the Mental Lives of Savages and Neurotics." In *The Standard Edition of the Complete Psychological Works of Sigmund Freud*, XIII: vii–162.
5. Reis, B. (In Press). Freud's Animality. *International Journal of Psychoanalysis*.
6. Tedeschi, J., and Tedeschi, A. (1990). "Clues: Roots of an Evidential Paradigm." In *Myths, Emblems, and the Historical Method.* Baltimore: Johns Hopkins University Press.
7. Tedeschi, J., and Tedeschi, A. (1990). "Clues: Roots of an Evidential Paradigm." In *Myths, Emblems, and the Historical Method.* Baltimore: Johns Hopkins University Press, p. 102.
8. Beer, G. (1983). *Darwin's Plots: Evolutionary Narrative in Darwin, George Eliot and Nineteenth Century Fiction.* London: Routledge & Kegan Paul.

9. Levine, G. (1988). *Darwin and the Novelists: Patterns of Science in Victorian Fiction*. Cambridge, MA: Harvard University Press.
10. Cited in Phillips, J., and Morley, J. (2003). *Imagination and Its Pathologies*. Cambridge, MA: MIT Press, p. 55.
11. Harari, Y. (2015). *Sapiens: A Brief History of Humankind*. New York: HarperCollins.
12. Taylor, C. (2004). *Modern Social Imaginaries*. Duke University Press.
13. Horowitz, M. (1972). Modes of Representation of Thought. *Journal of the American Psychoanalytic Association* 20: 793–819.
14. Blechner, M. (2018). *The Mindbrain and Dreams*. London and New York: Routledge.
15. Brann, E. (1991). *The World of the Imagination*. Rowman & Littlefield.
16. Lakoff, G., and Johnson, M. (1999). *Philosophy in the Flesh: The Embodied Mind and Its Challenge to Western Thought*. New York: Basic Books.
17. Healy, D. (1996). *The Bend for Home*. London: Harvill Press, p. 57.
18. Young, K. (1930). "Language and Social Interaction." In *Social Psychology: An Analysis of Social Behavior*. New York: Alfred A. Knopf (1930), Chapter 10, p. 205.
19. Sharpe, E.F. (1940). Psycho-Physical Problems Revealed in Language: An Examination of Metaphor. *International Journal of Psychoanalysis* 21: 202–3.
20. Loewald, H. (1978). "Primary Process, Secondary Process, and Language." In *Papers on Psychoanalysis*. New Haven: Yale University Press, 1980, pp. 178–206, p. 185.
21. Loewald, H. (1978). "Primary Process, Secondary Process, and Language." In *Papers on Psychoanalysis*. New Haven: Yale University Press, 1980, pp. 178–206, p. 197.
22. Vivona, J. (2006). From Developmental Metaphor to Developmental Model: The Shrinking Role of Language in the Talking Cure. *Journal of the American Psychoanalytic Association* 54: 877–902.
23. Cited in Loewald, H. (1978). *Papers on Psychoanalysis*. New Haven, CT: Yale University Press, 1980, p. 204.
24. Winnicott, D.W. (1949). "Mind and Its Relation to the Psyche-Soma." In *Through Paediatrics to Psycho-Analysis*. New York: Basic Books, 1975, pp. 243–54, p. 244.
25. Winnicott, D.W. (1965). "Communicating and Not Communicating Leading to a study of Certain Opposites." In *The Maturational Process and the Facilitating Environment*. London: Hogarth, p. 188, italics added.
26. Muller, J.P., and Richardson, W.J. (1982). *Lacan and Language: A Reader's Guide to Écrits*. New York: International Universities Press, p. 400.
27. Bakhtin, M.M. (1981). *The Dialogic Imagination*, ed. M. Holquist, trans. C. Emerson and M. Holquist. Austin, TX: University of Texas Press.
28. Lakoff, G., and Johnson, M. (1999). *Philosophy in the Flesh: The Embodied Mind and Its Challenge to Western Thought*. New York: Basic Books, p. 45.
29. Cited in Lewis, M. (2016). *The Undoing Project: A Friendship That Changed Our Minds*. W.W. Norton. Kindle edition, pp. 315–6.
30. Brooks, P. (2022). *Seduced by Story: The Use and Abuse of Narrative*. New York: The New York Review of Books.
31. Frost, R. (1930). "Education by Poetry." In *Robert Frost: Collected Poems, Prose and Plays*, ed. R. Poirier and M. Richardson. New York: Library of America, 1995, pp. 717–28.
32. Quoted in Gussow, M. (2000). "Interview with Yehuda Amichai." *New York Times*, September 23, p. A14.
33. Sandburg, C. (1916). *Chicago Poems*. New York: Henry Holt. (and Stilwell, KS: Digireads.com Publishing, p. 36.)
34. Vivona, J. (2003). Embracing Figures of Speech. *Psychoanalytic Psychology* 20 (1): 52–66.
35. Robinson, G., and Rundell, J. (1994). *Rethinking Imagination: Culture and Creativity*. London and New York: Routledge, p. 121.

36. Ogden, T. (2010). On Three Forms of Thinking. *Psychoanalytic Quarterly* LXXIX(2): 317–47, p. 319.
37. Ogden, T. (2010). On Three Forms of Thinking. *Psychoanalytic Quarterly* LXXIX(2): 317–47, p. 328.
38. Quinodoz, D. (2003). Words That Touch. *International Journal of Psychoanalysis* 84(6): 1469–85, p. 1475.
39. Frost, R. (1930). "Education by Poetry." In *Robert Frost: Collected Poems, Prose and Plays*, ed. R. Poirier and M. Richardson. New York: Library of America, 1995, p. 723.

Chapter 3 Night Tree Silhouettes

1. Pruyser, P. (1983). *The Play of Imagination: Toward a Psychoanalysis of Culture*. New York: International University Press, pp. 5–6.
2. Pruyser, P. (1983). *The Play of Imagination: Toward a Psychoanalysis of Culture*. New York: International University Press, p. 6.
3. Makin, S. (2020). "Born Ready: Babies Are Prewired to Perceive the World," *Scientific American*, March 2. www.scientificamerican.com/article/born-ready-babies-are-prewired-to-perceive-the-world/
4. Sagan, C. (1995). *The Demon-Haunted World: Science as a Candle in the Dark*. New York: Random House, p. 45.
5. Wordsworth, W. (1805). "The Prelude." In *William Wordsworth: The Major Works*, ed. S. Gill. New York: Oxford University Press, 2008, p. 398.
6. Coleridge, S.T. (1817). *Biographia Literaria*, ed. J. Engell and W.J. Bate. Princeton, NJ: Princeton University Press, 1983, p. 202.
7. Coleridge, S.T. (1802). "Dejection: An Ode." In *The Complete Poems*, ed. W. Keach. London: Penguin, 1997, p. 310.
8. Wordsworth, W. (1798). "Lines Written a Few Miles Above Tintern Abbey." In *William Wordsworth: The Major Works, Including the Prelude*, ed. S. Gill. New York: Oxford University Press, 2008, p. 134.
9. Cited in Warnock, M. (1978). *Imagination*. Berkeley, CA: University of California Press, pp. 118–9.
10. Cited in D'Agata, J. (2016). *The Making of the American Essay*. Minneapolis, MN: Graywolf Press, p. 351.
11. D'Agata, J. (2016). *The Making of the American Essay*. Minneapolis, MN: Graywolf Press, p. 352.
12. Nin, A. (1961). *Seduction of the Minotaur*. Chicago: The Swallow Press, p. 124.
13. Wright, K. (2009). Mirroring and Attunement: self-realization in psychoanalysis and art. Routledge, pp. 58–9.
14. Stevens, M., and Swan, A. (2004). *de Kooning: An American Master*. New York: Knopf, p. 571.
15. Woolf, V. (1985). "A Sketch of the Past." In *Moments of Being*. San Diego, New York, London: A Harvest Book, Harcourt, p. 72.
16. Goldman, D. (2017). *A Beholder's Share: Essays on Winnicott and the Psychoanalytic Imagination*. London and New York: Routledge.
17. Langer, S. (1953). *Feeling and Form*. London: Routledge & Kegan Paul, p. 40.
18. Wright, K. (2009). *Mirroring and Attunement: Self-Realization in Psychoanalysis and Art*. Hove, UK: Routledge, p. 65.
19. Milner, M. (1952). Aspects of Symbolism in Comprehension of the Not-Self. *International Journal of Psychoanalysis* 33: 181–94, p. 186.
20. Wright, K. (2009). *Mirroring and Attunement: Self-Realization in Psychoanalysis and Art*. Hove, UK: Routledge, p. 8.

21. Sontag, S. (1986). "Notes on 'Camp.'" In *Against Interpretation and Other Essays*. Picador Press, 2001, pp. 275–92, p. 276.
22. Sontag, S. (1986). "Notes on 'Camp.'" In *Against Interpretation and Other Essays*. Picador Press, 2001, pp. 275–92, p. 276.
23. See "Brief Manifesto: Mark Rothko with Adolph Gottlieb, and Barnett Newman," June 13, 1943, https://proussado.medium.com/brief-manifesto-mark-rothko-with-adolph-gottlieb-and-barnett-newman-bf01650381d1
24. Sontag, S. (1975). "Fascinating Fascism." *New York Review of Books*, February 6.

Chapter 4 Baby New to Earth and Sky

1. Balint, M. (1959). *Thrills and Regressions*. London: Hogarth Press, p. 62.
2. Ehrenzweig, A. (1971). The Hidden Order of Art. Berkeley and Los Angeles: University of California Press.
3. Freud, S. (1938). "Findings, Ideas, Problems." In The Standard Edition of the Complete Psychological Works of Sigmund Freud, XXIII: 299–300.
4. Winnicott, D.W. (1965). "Communicating and Not Communicating Leading to a Study of Certain Opposites." In The Maturational Process and the Facilitating Environment. London: Hogarth, p. 187.
5. Tennyson, A. (1850). "In Memoriam A.H.H.," Canto XLIV, www.online-literature.com/tennyson/718/
6. Balint, E. (1993). "Creative Life." In Before I Was I: Psychoanalysis and the Imagination, ed. J. Mitchell and M. Parsons, London: Free Association Books, p. 102.
7. Winnicott, D.W. (1945). "Primitive Emotional Development." In Through Paediatrics to Psycho-Analysis. New York: Basic Books, 1975, pp. 145–56, p. 153.
8. Winnicott, D.W. (1956). "Primary Maternal Preoccupation." In Through Paediatrics to Psycho-Analysis, New York: Basic Books, 1975, pp. 300–5.
9. Bashō, M. (1966). The Narrow Road to the Deep North and Other Travel Sketches. London: Penguin, p. 33.
10. Murdoch, I. (2014). The Sovereignty of Good. London and New York: Routledge, p. 82.
11. Roussillon, R. (2013). "The Deconstruction of Primary Narcissism." In Donald Winnicott Today, ed. J. Abram. London and New York: Routledge, p. 283
12. Roussillon, R. (2013). "The Deconstruction of Primary Narcissism." In Donald Winnicott Today, ed. J. Abram. London and New York: Routledge, p. 281
13. Ferutta, A. (2019). Winnicott's Research on "Becoming" in Personal Psychic Life: "My Latest Brain-Child." The Italian Psychoanalytic Annual (13): 121.
14. Wright, K. (1991). Vision and Separation: Between Mother and Baby. Northvale, NJ: Jason Aronson, p. xiii.
15. Piers, M.W. (ed.). (1972). Play and Development: A Symposium. New York: Norton, p. 54.
16. Erikson, E. (1977). Toys and Reasons: Stages in the Ritualization of Experience. New York: W.W. Norton, p. 47.
17. Loewald, H. (1971). "The Id and Regulatory Principles of Mental Functioning: A Discussion." In Papers on Psychoanalysis. New Haven: Yale University Press, 1980, p. 62.
18. Lear, J. (1996). The Introduction of Eros: Reflections on the Work of Hans Loewald. Journal of the American Psychoanalytic Association 44: 673–98.
19. Freud, S. (1920). "Beyond the Pleasure Principle." In The Standard Edition of the Complete Psychological Works of Sigmund Freud, XVIII: 1–64, p. 38.
20. Winnicott, D.W. (1964). "The Baby as a Going Concern." In The Child, the Family, and the *Outside World*. Harmondsworth, UK: Penguin, p. 27, italics added.

21. Descola, P. (2013). *Beyond Nature and Culture*. Chicago: University of Chicago Press.
22. Fox, S. (1981). *John Muir and His Legacy*. Boston: Little, Brown, p. 291.
23. Keller, H., Otto, H., Lamm, B., Yovsi, R.D., and Kärtner, J. (2008). "The Timing of Verbal/Vocal Communications Between Mothers and Their Infants: A Longitudinal Cross-Cultural Comparison." *Infant Behavior & Development* 31 (2), 217–26.

Chapter 5 Rama Playing

1. Adrain Plau, Manuscript Collections Information Analyst, Wellcome Collection, London, personal communication, August 8, 2023.
2. Stern, D.N. (2004). *The Present Moment in Psychotherapy and Everyday Life*. New York: W.W. Norton, p. 172–4.
3. Lyons-Ruth, K. (2000). I Sense That You Sense That I SENSE: Sander's Recognition Process and the Specificity of Relational Moves in the Psychotherapeutic Setting. *Infant Mental Health Journal* 21 (1–2): 85–98.
4. Winnicott, D.W. (1945). "Primitive Emotional Development." In *Through Paediatrics to Psycho-Analysis*. New York: Basic Books, 1975, pp. 145–56.
5. Sander, L. (1992). "Recognition Process: Organization and Specificity in Early Development: A Perspective on Developmental Process." Morton Levitt Memorial Lecture, University of California, Davis, April 21.
6. James Stoeri, PhD, personal communication.
7. Plato. (1988). *The Laws of Plato*, trans. Thomas L. Pangle. Chicago: University of Chicago Press, 673d.
8. Winnicott, D.W. (1964). "Why Children Play." In *The Child, the Family, and the Outside World*. Harmondsworth, UK: Penguin, pp. 134–8, p. 137.
9. Winnicott, D.W. (1964). "Why Children Play." In *The Child, the Family, and the Outside World*. Harmondsworth, UK: Penguin, pp. 134–8, p. 137.
10. Winnicott, D.W. (1986). *Home Is Where We Start From: Essays by a Psychoanalyst*, ed. C. Winnicott, R. Shepherd, and M. Davis, New York: W.W. Norton, p. 36.
11. Winnicott, D.W. (1988). *Human Nature*. New York: Schocken, p. 107.
12. Winnicott, D.W. (1968). "Communication Between Mother and Infant and Infant and Mother, Compared and Contrasted." In *Babies and Their Mothers*, ed. C. Winnicott, R. Shepherd, and M. Davis. Reading, MA: Addison-Wesley, 1987, p. 100.
13. Winnicott, D.W. (1988). *Human Nature*. New York: Schocken, p. 104.
14. Taipale, J. (2021). Being Carried Away. Fink and Winnicott on the Locus of Playing. *Journal of Phenomenological Psychology* 52: 193–217, p. 203.
15. Winnicott, D.W. (1971). *Playing and Reality*. Tavistock Publications, p. 67.
16. Winnicott, D.W. (1971). *Playing and Reality*. Tavistock Publications, p. 3.
17. Winnicott, D.W. (1971). *Playing and Reality*. Tavistock Publications, p. 55.
18. Brian Sutton-Smith quoted in Erikson, E. (1977). *Toys and Reasons: Stages in the Ritualization of Experience*. New York: W.W. Norton, p. 70.
19. Fast, I. (2012). The Primary Processes Grow Up: Freud's More Radical View of the Mind. *Contemporary Psychoanalysis* 48 (2): 183–98.
20. Vygotsky, L.S. (1978). *Mind in Society: The Development of Higher Psychological Processes*. Cambridge, MA: Harvard University Press, p. 102.
21. Fonagy, P. & Target, M. (1996). Playing With Reality: I. Theory of Mind and the Normal Development of Psychic Reality. *International Journal of Psychoanalysis* 77: 217–33.
22. Fonagy, P., Gergely, G., Jurist, E.L., and Target, M. (2002). *Affect Regulation, Mentalization, and the Development of the Self*. New York: Other Press.
23. Huizinga, J. (2016). *Homo Ludens: A Study of the Play Element in Culture*. Kettering, OH: Angelico Press, p. 8.

Chapter 6 What Do We Talk About When We Talk About Aggression?

1. Eve Lenert, personal communication.
2. Freud, S. (1930). "Civilization and Its Discontents." In *The Standard Edition of the Complete Psychological Works of Sigmund Freud*, XXI: 57–146, p. 110.
3. Alter, R. (2008). *The Five Books of Moses with Commentary*. New York: W.W. Norton, Chapter 6, Verse 5.
4. Fromm, E. (1991). *You Shall Be As Gods*. New York: Henry Holt, p. 126.
5. Freud, S. (1918). Letter from Sigmund Freud to Oskar Pfister, October 9, 1918. *Psychoanalysis and Faith: The Letters of Sigmund Freud and Oskar Pfister*, 59: 61–3. Psychoanalytic Electronic Publishing.
6. Freud, S. (1897). Letter 61 from "Extract from the Fliess Papers." In *The Standard Edition of the Complete Psychological Works of Sigmund Freud*, I: 247–8.
7. Freud, S. (1923). "The Ego and the Id." In *The Standard Edition of the Complete Psychological Works of Sigmund Freud*, XIX: 1–67, p. 26.
8. Freud, S. (1923). "The Ego and the Id." In *The Standard Edition of the Complete Psychological Works of Sigmund Freud*, XIX: 1–67, p. 26n.
9. Freud, S. (1905). "Three Essays on the Theory of Sexuality." In *The Standard Edition of the Complete Psychological Works of Sigmund Freud*, VII: 123–246, p. 197.
10. Abram, J., and Hinshelwood, R.D. (2018). *The Clinical Paradigms of Melanie Klein and Donald Winnicott: Comparisons and Dialogues*. London and New York: Routledge, p. 54.
11. Winnicott, D.W. (1971). "Creativity and Its Origins." In *Playing and Reality*. Tavistock Publications, p. 70.
12. Ibn Pekuda, *Duties of the Heart*. www.sefaria.org/Duties_of_the_Heart,_Fifth_Treatise_on_Devotion
13. See Wikipedia entry on Augustinianism. https://en.wikipedia.org/wiki/Augustinianism
14. Alvarez, A. (2011). "Which Violence and Whose Violence? Questions Arising in the Psychotherapy of Aggressive Children." In *Aggression: From Phantasy to Action*, ed. P. Williams. London: Karnac.
15. Winnicott, D.W. (1950–55). "Aggression in Relation to Emotional Development." In *Through Pediatrics to Psycho-Analysis*. London: Hogarth, 1975, pp. 204–18, p. 204.
16. Winnicott, D.W. (1988). *Human Nature*. New York: Schocken Books, p. 127.
17. Winnicott, D.W. (1967). "Postscript: D.W.W. on D.W.W." In *Psychoanalytic Explorations*. Cambridge, MA: Harvard University Press,1989, pp. 569–82, p. 574.
18. Winnicott, D.W. (1964). "Roots of Aggression." In *The Child, the Family, and the Outside World*. Harmondsworth: Penguin, p. 231.
19. Winnicott, D.W. (1964). "Roots of Aggression." In *The Child, the Family, and the Outside World*. Harmondsworth: Penguin, p. 231.
20. Winnicott, D.W. (1950–55). "Aggression in Relation to Emotional Development." In *Through Pediatrics to Psycho-Analysis*. London: Hogarth, 1975, pp. 204–18, p. 216.
21. Winnicott, D.W. (1950–55). "Aggression in Relation to Emotional Development." In *Through Pediatrics to Psycho-Analysis*. London: Hogarth, 1975, pp. 204–18, p. 205.
22. Winnicott, D.W. (1950–55). "Aggression in Relation to Emotional Development." In *Through Pediatrics to Psycho-Analysis*. London: Hogarth, 1975, pp. 204–18, p. 216.
23. Winnicott, D.W. (1950–55). "Aggression in Relation to Emotional Development." In *Through Pediatrics to Psycho-Analysis*. London: Hogarth, 1975, pp. 204–18, p. 215.
24. Winnicott, D.W. (1950–55). "Aggression in Relation to Emotional Development." In *Through Pediatrics to Psycho-Analysis*. London: Hogarth, 1975, pp. 204–18, p. 215.
25. Winnicott, D.W. (1950–55). "Aggression in Relation to Emotional Development." In *Through Pediatrics to Psycho-Analysis*. London: Hogarth, 1975, pp. 204–18, p. 210.

26. Winnicott, D.W. (1970). "Individuation." In *Psychoanalytic Explorations*. Cambridge, MA: Harvard University Press, 1989, pp. 284–8, p. 287.
27. Elkins, J. (2015). Motility, Aggression, and the Bodily I: An Interpretation of Winnicott. The Psychoanalytic Quarterly, Volume LXXXIV (4): 943–73.
28. Winnicott, D.W. (1949). "Birth Memories, Birth Trauma, and Anxiety." In *Through Pediatrics to Psycho-Analysis*. London: Hogarth, 1975, pp. 174–93, p. 186.
29. Winnicott, D.W. (1950–55). "Aggression in Relation to Emotional Development." In *Through Pediatrics to Psycho-Analysis*. London: Hogarth, 1975, pp. 204–18, p. 215, italics added.
30. Winnicott, D.W. (1950–55). "Aggression in Relation to Emotional Development." In *Through Pediatrics to Psycho-Analysis*. London: Hogarth, 1975, pp. 204–18, p. 212.
31. Winnicott, D.W. (1950–55). "Aggression in Relation to Emotional Development." In *Through Pediatrics to Psycho-Analysis*. London: Hogarth, 1975, pp. 204–18, p. 212.
32. Winnicott, D.W. (1950–55). "Aggression in Relation to Emotional Development." In *Through Pediatrics to Psycho-Analysis*. London: Hogarth, 1975, pp. 204–18, p. 216.
33. Winnicott, D.W. (1949). "Mind and Its Relation to the Psyche-Soma." In *Through Paediatrics to Psycho-Analysis*. New York: Basic Books, 1975, pp. 243–54, p. 244.
34. Winnicott, D.W. (1950–55). "Aggression in Relation to Emotional Development." In *Through Pediatrics to Psycho-Analysis*. London: Hogarth, 1975, pp. 204–18, p. 205.
35. Winnicott, D.W. (1950–55). "Aggression in Relation to Emotional Development." In *Through Pediatrics to Psycho-Analysis*. London: Hogarth, 1975, pp. 204–18, p. 211–2.
36. Winnicott, D.W. (1950–55). "Aggression in Relation to Emotional Development." In *Through Pediatrics to Psycho-Analysis*. London: Hogarth, 1975, pp. 204–18, p. 212.

Chapter 7 Magritte and the Use of an Object

1. Magritte, R. (2016). Interview with Louis Quiévreux. In *René Magritte: Selected Writings*, ed. K. Rooney and E. Plattner. Minneapolis, MN: University of Minnesota Press, p. 108.
2. Breton, A. (1924). Manifesto of Surrealism. www2.hawaii.edu/~freeman/courses/phil 330/MANIFESTO OF SURREALISM.pdf, italics added.
3. Breton, A. (1924). Manifesto of Surrealism. www2.hawaii.edu/~freeman/courses/phil 330/MANIFESTO OF SURREALISM.pdf, italics added.
4. Chao, S.-l. (2010). *Rethinking the Concept of the Grotesque: Crashaw, Baudelaire, Magritte*. London: Legenda, p. 165.
5. Magritte, R. (2016). *René Magritte: Selected Writings*, ed. K. Rooney and E. Plattner. Minneapolis, MN: University of Minnesota Press, p. 204.
6. Magritte, R. (2016). *René Magritte: Selected Writings*, ed. K. Rooney and E. Plattner. Minneapolis, MN: University of Minnesota Press, p. 204.
7. Magritte, R. (2016). *René Magritte: Selected Writings*, ed. K. Rooney and E. Plattner. Minneapolis, MN: University of Minnesota Press, p. xii.
8. Magritte, R. (2016). *René Magritte: Selected Writings*, ed. K. Rooney and E. Plattner. Minneapolis, MN: University of Minnesota Press, pp. xvii–xviii, original italics.
9. Magritte, R. (2016). *René Magritte: Selected Writings*, ed. K. Rooney and E. Plattner. Minneapolis, MN: University of Minnesota Press, p. 200.
10. Magritte, R. (2016). *René Magritte: Selected Writings*, ed. K. Rooney and E. Plattner. Minneapolis, MN: University of Minnesota Press, p. 92.
11. Barron, S., Draguet, M., and Tashjiian, D. (2006). *Magritte and Contemporary Art: The Treachery of Images*. Ludion/Los Angeles County Museum of Art.
12. Abram, J. (2022). *The Surviving Object: Psychoanalytic Clinical Essays on Psychic Survival-of-the-Object*. Abingdon, UK: Routledge, p. xxiv.

13. Abram, J. (2022). *The Surviving Object: Psychoanalytic Clinical Essays on Psychic Survival-of-the-Object*. Abingdon, UK: Routledge, p. 2.
14. Winnicott, D.W. (1969). The Use of an Object. *International Journal of Psychoanalysis* 50: 711–16, p. 713.
15. Winnicott, D.W. (1969). The Use of an Object. *International Journal of Psychoanalysis* 50: 711–16, p. 714.
16. Winnicott, D.W. (1953). Transitional Objects and Transitional Phenomena: A Study of the First Not-Me Possession. *International Journal of Psychoanalysis* XXXIV (2): 89–97, p. 91.
17. Winnicott, D.W. (1950–55). "Aggression in Relation to Emotional Development." In *Through Pediatrics to Psycho-Analysis*. London: Hogarth, 1975, pp. 204–18, p. 216.
18. Winnicott, D.W. (1950–55). "Aggression in Relation to Emotional Development." In *Through Pediatrics to Psycho-Analysis*. London: Hogarth, 1975, pp. 204–18, p. 212, italics in original.
19. Winnicott, D.W. (1949). "Mind and Its Relation to the Psyche-Soma." In *Through Paediatrics to Psycho-Analysis*. New York: Basic Books, 1975, pp. 243–54, p. 244.
20. Winnicott, D.W. (1988). *Human Nature*. New York: Schocken Books, p. 104.
21. Winnicott, D.W. (1952). "Psychosis and Child Care." In *Through Pediatrics to Psycho-Analysis*. London: Hogarth, 1975, pp. 219–28, pp. 222–3, italics added.
22. Winnicott, D.W. (1969). The Use of an Object. *International Journal of Psychoanalysis* 50: 711–16, p. 712.
23. Winnicott, D.W. (1948). "Pediatrics and Psychiatry." In *Through Pediatrics to Psycho-Analysis*. London: Hogarth, 1975, pp. 157–73, p. 163.
24. Winnicott, D.W. (1986). *Home Is Where We Start From: Essays by a Psychoanalyst*, ed. C. Winnicott, R. Shepherd, and M. Davis, New York: W.W. Norton, p. 40.
25. Winnicott, D.W. (1988). *Human Nature*. New York: Schocken Books, p. 79.
26. Winnicott, D.W. (1969). The Use of an Object. *International Journal of Psychoanalysis* 50: 711–16, p. 714.
27. Winnicott, D.W. (1941). "The Observation of Infants in a Set Situation." In *Through Pediatrics to Psycho-Analysis*. London: Hogarth, 1975, pp. 52–69.
28. Winnicott, D.W. (1963). "D.W.W's Dream Related to Reviewing Jung." In *Psychoanalytic Explorations*. Cambridge, MA: Harvard University Press, 1989, pp. 228–30, p. 230, italics added.
29. Eliot, T.S. (1922). *The Waste-Land*. www.poetryfoundation.org/poems/47311/the-waste-land
30. Winnicott, D.W. (1969). The Use of an Object. *International Journal of Psychoanalysis* 50: 711–16, p. 714.
31. Winnicott, D.W. (1968). "Comments on My Paper 'The Use of an Object.'" In *Psychoanalytic Explorations*. Cambridge, MA: Harvard University Press, 1989, pp. 238–40, pp. 239–40.
32. Winnicott, D.W. (1969). "The Use of an Object in the Context of Moses and Monotheism." In *Psychoanalytic Explorations*. Cambridge, MA: Harvard University Press, 1989, pp. 240–46, p. 245, italics in original.
33. Winnicott, D.W. (1969). "The Use of an Object in the Context of Moses and Monotheism." In *Psychoanalytic Explorations*. Cambridge, MA: Harvard University Press, 1989, pp. 240–46, p. 246.
34. Winnicott, D.W. (1968). "Comments on My Paper 'The Use of an Object.'" In *Psychoanalytic Explorations*. Cambridge, MA: Harvard University Press, 1989, pp. 238–40, p. 239.
35. Frye, N. (1969). *The Anatomy of Criticism*. New York: Atheneum, p. 334.
36. Kearney, R. (1988). *The Wake of Imagination*. Minneapolis, MN: University of Minnesota Press, p. 80.

37. Donoghue, D. (1973). *Thieves of Fire*. London: Faber, p. 26.
38. Donoghue, D. (1973). *Thieves of Fire*. London: Faber, p. 26.
39. Kearney, R. (1988). *The Wake of Imagination*. Minneapolis, MN: University of Minnesota Press, p. 106.
40. Winnicott, D.W. (1969). "The Use of an Object in the Context of Moses and Monotheism." In *Psychoanalytic Explorations*. Cambridge, MA: Harvard University Press, 1989, pp. 240–46, p. 245.
41. Balint, E. (1963). "On Being Empty of Oneself." In Balint, E. (1993). *Before I Was I: Psychoanalysis and the Imagination*, ed. J. Mitchell and M. Parsons. London: Free Association Books, p. 51.
42. Wright, K. (2009). *Mirroring and Attunement: Self-Realization in Psychoanalysis and Art*. Hove, UK: Routledge, p. 4.
43. Gombrich, E.H. (1960). *Art and Illusion: A Study in the Psychology of Pictorial Representation*. New York: Pantheon Books, p. 211.

Chapter 8 Are We Virtuoso Storytellers?

1. Kearney, R. (2002). *On Stories*. London: Routledge, p. 5.
2. Kearney, R. (2002). *On Stories*. London: Routledge, p. 4.
3. Kearney, R. (2002). *On Stories*. London: Routledge, p. 4.
4. Bruner, J. (1994). "The 'Remembered' Self." In *The Remembering Self: Construction and Accuracy in the Self-Narrative*, ed. U. Neisser and R. Fivush. Cambridge University Press. p. 53.
5. Bruner, J. (1987). Life as Narrative. *Social Research*, Vol 54, No. 1, pp. 11–32, p. 15.
6. Taylor, C. (1989). *Sources of the Self*. Cambridge University Press, p. 47.
7. Brooks, P. (2022). *Seduced by Story: The Use and Abuse of Narrative*. New York: The New York Review of Books, pp. 7–8.
8. MacIntyre, A. (1981). *After Virtue: A Study in Moral Theory*. University of Notre Dame Press. First edition, p. 216.
9. Eliot, G. (1990). "The Natural History of German Life." In *Selected Essays, Poems, and Other Writings*. London: Penguin Classics, p. 110.
10. Healy, D. (1996). *The Bend for Home*. London: Harvill Press, p. 57.
11. Spence, D.P. (1982). *Narrative Truth and Historical Truth: Meaning and Interpretation in Psychoanalysis*. New York: W.W. Norton.
12. Cited in Strawson, G. (2018). *Things That Bother Me: Death, Freedom, the Self, etc.* New York: New York Review Books, Kindle edition, location 458.
13. Emerson, R.W. (1841). Circles. https://emersoncentral.com/texts/essays-first-series/circles/
14. Borges, J.L. (1964). "Borges and I." In *Labyrinths: Selected Stories & Other Writings*. New York: New Directions, pp. 246–7, p. 246.
15. James, H. (1879). Letter to William James. February 23, 1879. Houghton Library, Harvard University, italics added.
16. Bakhtin, M.M. (1981). *The Dialogic Imagination*, ed. M. Holquist, trans. C. Emerson and M. Holquist. Austin, TX: University of Texas Press.
17. Pontalis, J.-B. (1993). *Love of Beginnings*. Cited in Phillips, A. (1994). *On Flirtation: Psychoanalytic Essays on the Uncommitted Life*. Cambridge, MA: Harvard University Press, p. 73.
18. Wood, J. (2015). *The Nearest Thing to Life*. Brandeis University Press, p. 37, italics added.
19. Boswell, R. (2008). *The Half-Known World: On Writing Fiction*. Minneapolis, MN.: Graywolf Press, p. 100.

20. Boswell, R. (2008). *The Half-Known World: On Writing Fiction.* Minneapolis, MN.: Graywolf Press, p. 15.
21. Boswell, R. (2008). *The Half-Known World: On Writing Fiction.* Minneapolis, MN.: Graywolf Press, p. 102, italics added.
22. Freud, S. (1937). "Constructions in Analysis." In *The Standard Edition of the Complete Psychological Works of Sigmund Freud,* XXIII: 255–70, p. 258.
23. Phillips, A. (1994). *On Flirtation: Psychoanalytic Essays on the Uncommitted Life.* Cambridge, MA: Harvard University Press, p. 69.
24. Freud, S. (1914). "Remembering, Repeating, and Working Through." In *The Standard Edition of the Complete Psychological Works of Sigmund Freud,* XII: 145–56, p. 154.
25. Brooks, P. (1994). *Psychoanalysis as Storytelling.* Cambridge, MA: Blackwell, p. 53.
26. Cited in Phillips, A. (1994). *On Flirtation: Psychoanalytic Essays on the Uncommitted Life.* Cambridge, MA: Harvard University Press, p. 73.
27. Freud, S. (1899). "Screen Memories." In *The Standard Edition of the Complete Psychological Works of Sigmund Freud,* III: 299–322, p. 306.
28. Freud, S. (1899). "Screen Memories." In *The Standard Edition of the Complete Psychological Works of Sigmund Freud,* III: 299–322, p. 322.
29. Wittgenstein, L., and Rhees, R. (1968). Conversations on Freud. *Psychoanalytic Review* 55: 376–86, pp. 376–7.
30. Winnicott, D.W. (1971). "The Place Where We Live." In *Playing and Reality.* Tavistock Publications, pp. 104–10, p. 109.
31. Bowie, M. (1993). *Psychoanalysis and the Future of Theory.* Oxford and Cambridge, MA: Blackwell, p. 127.
32. Bowie, M. (1993). *Psychoanalysis and the Future of Theory.* Oxford and Cambridge, MA: Blackwell, p. 98.
33. Winnicott, D.W. (1971). "Playing: Creative Activity and the Search for the Self." In *Playing and Reality.* Tavistock, pp. 53–64, pp. 55–6.
34. Winnicott, D.W. (1960). "The Theory of Parent–Infant Relationship." In *The Collected Works of D.W. Winnicott: Vol 6: 1960–1963,* ed. L. Caldwell & H. Taylor Robinson. Oxford: Oxford University Press, pp. 141–58, p. 147.
35. Stern, D.N. (2004). *The Present Moment in Psychotherapy and Everyday Life.* New York: W.W. Norton, p. 55.
36. Stern, D.N. (2004). *The Present Moment in Psychotherapy and Everyday Life.* New York: W.W. Norton, p. 55.
37. Woolf, V. (1985). "A Sketch of the Past." In *Moments of Being.* San Diego, New York, and London: A Harvest Book, Harcourt, pp. 61–160.
38. Stern, D.N. (2004). *The Present Moment in Psychotherapy and Everyday Life.* New York: W.W. Norton, p. 58.
39. Stern, D.N. (2004). *The Present Moment in Psychotherapy and Everyday Life.* New York: W.W. Norton, p. 55.
40. Wood, J. (2015). *The Nearest Thing to Life.* Brandeis University Press, p. 36.
41. Eliot, T.S. (2023). "Burnt Norton." Number 1 in *Four Quartets: A Poem.* Ecco.
42. Levine, H.B., Reed, G.S., and Scarfone, D. (2013). *Unrepresented States and the Construction of Meaning: Clinical and Theoretical Contributions.* London: Karnac Books.
43. McGilchrist, I. (2009). *The Master and his Emissary: The Divided Brain and the Making of the Western World.* New Haven, CT: Yale University Press.
44. Balint, E. (1993). *Before I Was I: Psychoanalysis and the Imagination,* ed. J. Mitchell and M. Parsons. London: Free Association Books.
45. Bromberg, P. (1998). *Standing in the Spaces: Essays on Clinical Process, Trauma, and Dissociation.* Hillsdale, NJ: The Analytic Press.
46. Stern, D.N. (1985). *The Interpersonal World of the Infant.* New York: Basic Books, p. 98.

47. Stern, D.N. (1985). *The Interpersonal World of the Infant*. New York: Basic Books, p. 111.
48. Interview with Nan Goldin in documentary movie *All the Beauty and the Bloodshed*.
49. van den Kolk, B. (2015). *The Body Keeps the Score: Brain, Mind, and Body in the Healing of Trauma*. Penguin.
50. Caruth, C. (ed.) (1995). *Trauma: Explorations in Memory*. Baltimore and London: Johns Hopkins University Press, p. 5.
51. Caruth, C. (2016). *Unclaimed Experience: Trauma, Narrative, and History*. Baltimore and London: Johns Hopkins University Press.
52. Winnicott, D.W. (1974). Fear of Breakdown. *International Review of Psychoanalysis* 1: 103–7, p. 106.
53. Caruth, C. (ed.) (1995). *Trauma: Explorations in Memory*. Baltimore and London: Johns Hopkins University Press, p. 5.
54. Caruth, C. (ed.) (1995). *Trauma: Explorations in Memory*. Baltimore and London: Johns Hopkins University Press, p. 153.
55. Caruth, C. (ed.) (1995). *Trauma: Explorations in Memory*. Baltimore and London: Johns Hopkins University Press, p. 154, italics in original.
56. Lanzmann, C. (1995). "The Obscenity of Understanding: An Evening With Claude Lanzmann." In *Trauma: Explorations in Memory*, ed. C. Caruth. Baltimore and London: Johns Hopkins University Press, p. 204.
57. Freud, S. (1926). "Inhibitions, Symptoms, and Anxiety." In *The Standard Edition of the Complete Psychological Works of Sigmund Freud*, XX: 77–178, p. 169.
58. Freud, S. (1917). "Mourning and Melancholia." In *The Standard Edition of the Complete Psychological Works of Sigmund Freud*, XIV: 237–58.
59. Bion, W. (1970). *Attention and Interpretation*. London: Maresfield Library, p. 19.
60. Cited in Robinson, G., and Rundell, J. (1994). *Rethinking Imagination: Culture and Creativity*. London and New York: Routledge, p. 137.
61. Bion, W.R. (1962). "The Psycho-Analytic Study of Thinking." *International Journal of Psychoanalysis* 43: 306–310, p. 309.
62. Winnicott, D.W. (1988). *Human Nature*. New York: Schocken Books, p. 80.

Chapter 9 "But She Talks Just Like I Write"

1. Gilbert, S., and Ellman, R. (eds.). (1966). *Letters of James Joyce*, Vol. 1. New York: The Viking Press, p. 166.
2. Gilbert, S., and Ellman, R. (eds.). (1966). *Letters of James Joyce*, Vol. 1. New York: The Viking Press, p. 166. See also, Spender, S. (1957). The Daytime World of James Joyce. New York Times Books, May 26. https://archive.nytimes.com/www.nytimes.com/books/00/01/09/specials/joyce-letters.html
3. Menand, L. (2012). Silence, Exile, Punning. *The New Yorker*, June 25. www.newyorker.com/magazine/2012/07/02/silence-exile-punning
4. Menand, L. (2012). Silence, Exile, Punning. *The New Yorker*, June 25. www.newyorker.com/magazine/2012/07/02/silence-exile-punning
5. Menand, L. (2012). Silence, Exile, Punning. *The New Yorker*, June 25. www.newyorker.com/magazine/2012/07/02/silence-exile-punning
6. Menand, L. (2012). Silence, Exile, Punning. *The New Yorker*, June 25. www.newyorker.com/magazine/2012/07/02/silence-exile-punning
7. Ellmann, R. (1982). *James Joyce*. London: Oxford University Press, Preface.
8. Cited in Menand, L. (2012). Silence, Exile, Punning. *The New Yorker*, June 25. www.newyorker.com/magazine/2012/07/02/silence-exile-punning
9. Cited in Wood, J. (2015). *The Nearest Thing to Life*. Brandeis University Press, p. 39.
10. 10, James Stoeri, personal communication.

11. Kearney, R. (2002). *On Stories*. London: Routledge, p. 19.
12. Hutchins, P. (1957). *James Joyce's World*. North Yorkshire: Methuen, p. 184.
13. Hutchins, P. (1957). *James Joyce's World*. North Yorkshire: Methuen, p. 185.
14. Cited in Lee, H. (2003). "No She Said No." Review of "Lucia Joyce: To Dance in the Wake," by Carol Loeb Shloss. *New York Times Book Review*, December 28. www.nytimes.com/2003/12/28/books/no-she-said-no.html
15. Cited in Lee, H. (2003). "No She Said No." Review of "Lucia Joyce: To Dance in the Wake," by Carol Loeb Shloss. *New York Times Book Review*, December 28. www.nytimes.com/2003/12/28/books/no-she-said-no.html
16. Ellmann, R. (1982). *James Joyce*. London: Oxford University Press, p. 622.
17. Joyce, J. (2022). *Portrait of an Artist as a Young Man*. Ottawa, Canada: East India Publishing, p. 153, italics added.
18. Joyce, J. (2022). *Portrait of an Artist as a Young Man*. Ottawa, Canada: East India Publishing, p. 197.
19. Hutchins, P. (1957). *James Joyce's World*. North Yorkshire: Methuen, p. 185.
20. Cited in Ellmann, R. (1982). *James Joyce*. London: Oxford University Press, p. 663.
21. Menand, L. (2012). Silence, Exile, Punning. *The New Yorker*, June 25. www.newyorker.com/magazine/2012/07/02/silence-exile-punning

Chapter 10 Paracosms in the Parsonage

1. Harman, C. (2017). *Charlotte Brontë: A Fiery Heart*. New York: Vintage Books, p. 79.
2. Beehler, B. (2022). Charolette Brontë's Paper Dolls. *ELH Journal* 89 (1, Spring). https://muse.jhu.edu/article/848857
3. Alexander, C. (2010). *Tales of Glass Town, Angria, and Gondal: Selected Early Writings*. Oxford: Oxford University Press, p. xvi.
4. Alexander, C. (2010). *Tales of Glass Town, Angria, and Gondal: Selected Early Writings*. Oxford: Oxford University Press, p. xvi.
5. Silvey, R., and MacKeith, S. (1988). "The Paracosm: A Special form of Phantasy." In *Organizing Early Experience: Imagination and Cognition in Childhood*, ed. D. Morrison. Amityville, NY: Baywood, pp. 173–97, p. 174.
6. Morrison, D., and Morrison, S.L. (2006). *Memories of Loss and Dreams of Perfection: Unsuccessful Childhood Grieving and Adult Creativity*. Amityville, NY: Baywood, p. 1.
7. Morrison, D., and Morrison, S.L. (2006). *Memories of Loss and Dreams of Perfection: Unsuccessful Childhood Grieving and Adult Creativity*. Amityville, NY: Baywood, pp. 1–2.
8. Morrison, D., and Morrison, S.L. (2006). *Memories of Loss and Dreams of Perfection: Unsuccessful Childhood Grieving and Adult Creativity*. Amityville, NY: Baywood, p. 21.
9. Morrison, D., and Morrison, S.L. (2006). *Memories of Loss and Dreams of Perfection: Unsuccessful Childhood Grieving and Adult Creativity*. Amityville, NY: Baywood, p. 20.
10. Blom, M.A. (1975). Apprenticeship in "The World Below": Charlotte Brontë's Juvenilia. *ESC: English Studies in Canada* 1 (3): 290–303.   Project MUSE. doi.org/10.1353/esc.1975.0028
11. Morrison, D. and Morrison, S.L (2006). *Memories of Loss and Dreams of Perfection: Unsuccessful Childhood Grieving and Adult Creativity*. Amityville, NY: Baywood, p. 71.
12. Root-Bernstein, M. (2014). *Inventing Imaginary Worlds: From Childhood Play to Adult Creativity Across the Arts and Sciences*. Roman & Littlefield.
13. Dewey, J. (1934). *Art as Experience*. New York: Perigee Books, p. 272.

14. Cited in Silvey, R., and MacKeith, S. (1988). "The Paracosm: A Special form of Phantasy." In *Organizing Early Experience: Imagination and Cognition in Childhood*, ed. D. Morrison. Amityville, NY: Baywood, pp. 173–97, p. 191.

15. Alexander, C. (2010). *Tales of Glass Town, Angria, and Gondal: Selected Early Writings*. Oxford: Oxford University Press, pp. 6–7.

16. Taylor, C. (2004). *Modern Social Imaginaries*. Duke University Press, p. 23, italics added.

17. Cited in Thompson, J.B. (1985). *Studies in the Theory of Ideology*. Berkeley, CA: Universilty of California Press, p. 24, italics added.

18. Laing, R.D. (1969). *Self and Others*. London: Tavistock, pp. 38–40.

19. Lacan, J. (1997). *Écrits: A Selection*. London: Routledge, p. 21, italics added.

20. Gopnik, Adam (2002, September 30). Bumping Into Mr. Ravioli. *The New Yorker*, 78 (29): 80.

21. Taylor, M. (1999). *Imaginary Companions and the Children Who Create Them*. New York: Oxford University Press.

22. Gopnik, A. (2009). *The Philosophical Baby: What Children's Minds Tell Us About Truth, Love, and the Meaning of Life*. New York: Picador, p. 54.

23. Gopnik, A. (2009). *The Philosophical Baby: What Children's Minds Tell Us About Truth, Love, and the Meaning of Life*. New York: Picador, p. 52.

24. Cross, C. (2019). *Heavier Than Heaven: The Biography of Kurt Cobain*. London: Hodder & Stoughton.

25. Margaritoff, M. (2023). Inside the Text of Kurt Cobain's Heart Wrenching Suicide Note. *All That's Interesting* (ATI). June 4.   https://allthatsinteresting.com/kurt-cob ain-suicide-note

26. Taylor, M. (1999). *Imaginary Companions and the Children Who Create Them*. New York: Oxford University Press.

27. Alexander, C. (2010). *Tales of Glass Town, Angria, and Gondal: Selected Early Writings*. Oxford: Oxford University Press, pp. 6–7.

28. Alexander, C. (2006). *The Oxford Companion to the Brontës*. Oxford: Oxford University Press.

29. Stoeri, J. (2005). Surprise, Shock, and Dread, and the Nature of Therapeutic Action. *Contemporary Psychoanalysis* 41: 183–202.

30. Bowen, J., and Dinsdale, A. (n.d.). The Brontës' Early Writings: Combining Phantasy and Fact. British Library Video. www.YouTube.com/watch?v=0Z01Bzs0Dqo

31. Bowen, J., and Dinsdale, A. (n.d.). The Brontës' Early Writings: Combining Phantasy and Fact. British Library Video. www.YouTube.com/watch?v=0Z01Bzs0Dqo

32. Ratchford, F.E. (1949). *The Brontës Web of Childhood*. New York: Columbia University Press, p. 105.

33. Winnicott, D.W. (1971). *Playing and Reality*. Tavistock, p. 27.

34. Stevens, W. (1990). "Holiday in Reality." In *The Collected Poems of Wallace Stevens*. U.S. Vintage reissue edition, p. 313.

35. Brontë, C. (1830). The Poetaster: A Drama by Lord Charles Wellesley, Charlotte Brontë, Relating to the Young Men, Play in Two Volumes [Haworth]: Autograph Manuscript Signed, 1830 June 8–July 12.   Morgan Library, Literary and Historical Manuscripts (LHMS), http://corsair.themorgan.org/vwebv/holdingsInfo?bibId=81845

36. Bowen, J., and Dinsdale, A. (n.d.). The Brontës' Early Writings: Combining Phantasy and Fact. British Library Video. www.YouTube.com/watch?v=0Z01Bzs0Dqo

37. Du Maurier, D. (1961). *The Infernal World of Branwell Brontë*. Garden City, NY: Doubleday.

38. Barker, J. (1994). *The Brontes*. London: Weidenfeld & Nicolson.

39. Lane, M. (1980). *The Drug-Like Brontë Dream*. London: John Murray, p. 19.

40. Cited in Barker, J. (1997). *The Brontës: A Life in Letters*. New York: Overlook Press, p. 47.

41. Hatfield, C.W. (ed.). (1941). *The Complete Poems of Emily Jane Brontë.* New York: Columbia University Press.
42. Marsden, S. (2014). *Emily Brontë and the Religious Imagination.* London: Bloomsbury.
43. Rycroft, C. (1968). *Imagination and Reality.* New York: International Universities Press, p. 37.
44. Barker, J. (1994). *The Brontes.* London: Weidenfeld & Nicolson, p. 195.
45. Gérin, W. (1971). *Emily Brontë.* Oxford: Clarendon Press, p. 242.
46. Morrison, D. and Morrison, S.L (2006). *Memories of Loss and Dreams of Perfection: Unsuccessful Childhood Grieving and Adult Creativity.* Amityville, NY: Baywood, p. 77.
47. Alexander, C. (2018, July 4). In Search of the Authorial Self: Branwell Brontë's Microcosmic World. *Journal of Juvenilia Studies* 1: 3–19, p. 7.   doi:10.29173/jjs126. ISSN 2561-8326
48. Alexander, C. (2018, July 4). In Search of the Authorial Self: Branwell Brontë's Microcosmic World. *Journal of Juvenilia Studies* 1: 3–19, p. 11.
49. Alexander, C. (2018, July 4). In Search of the Authorial Self: Branwell Brontë's Microcosmic World. *Journal of Juvenilia Studies* 1: 3–19, p. 16.
50. Du Maurier, D. (1961). *The Infernal World of Branwell Brontë.* Garden City, NY: Doubleday, Publisher's blurb.
51. Cohen, B. (2013). "The Dissociative Reality." In *Handbook of Dissociation: Theoretical, Empirical, and Clinical Perspectives,* ed. L. Michelson and W.J. Ray. Springer Science and Business Media, p. 533.
52. Bentley, P.E. (1969). *The Brontes and Their World.* London: Thames & Hudson.
53. Barker, J, (1994). *The Brontes.* London: Weidenfeld & Nicolson, pp. 139–40.
54. Winnicott, D.W. (1971). *Playing and Reality.* Tavistock, p. 54.
55. Winnicott, D.W. (1971). *Playing and Reality.* Tavistock, p. 55.
56. Barker, J. (1994). *The Brontes.* London: Weidenfeld & Nicolson, p. 237.
57. Barker, J. (1994). *The Brontes.* London: Weidenfeld & Nicolson, p. 547.

Coda

1. Bishop, E. (2006). "Writing Poetry Is an Unnatural Act …" In *Edgar Allan Poe & the Juke-Box: Uncollected Poems, Drafts, and Fragments.* New York: Farrar, Straus & Giroux, pp. 207–15, p. 212.
2. Paul Simon, (1973). "Kodachrome." ww.paulsimon.com/track/kodachrome-7/
3. Atwood, M. (2002). "Duplicity: The Jekyll Hand, the Hyde Hand, and the Slippery Double." In *Negotiating with the Dead: A Writer on Writing.* Anchor Books, pp. 56–7.
4. Cited in Eden, V. (2018). Life Remains on the Surface of Silence: Lea Goldberg's Last Poems. *World Literature Today.* March 28.   Online edition: www.worldliteratureto day.org/blog/book-reviews/life-remains-surface-silence-lea-goldbergs-last-poems-viv ian-eden
5. Winnicott, D.W. (1949). "Mind and Its Relation to the Psyche-Soma." In *Through Paediatrics to Psycho-Analysis.* New York: Basic Books, 1975, pp. 243–54.
6. Yeats, W.B. (1933). "A Prayer for Old Age." https://allpoetry.com/A-Prayer-For-Old-Age
7. Oliver, M. (1986) "Wild Geese." In *Dream Work.* New York: Grove/Atlantic, p. 347.

References

Abram, J. (2022). *The Surviving Object: Psychoanalytic Clinical Essays on Psychic Survival-of-the-Object*. Abingdon, UK: Routledge.

Abram, J., and Hinshelwood, R.D. (2018). *The Clinical Paradigms of Melanie Klein and Donald Winnicott: Comparisons and Dialogues*. London and New York: Routledge.

Alexander, C. (2006). *The Oxford Companion to the Brontës*. Oxford: Oxford University Press.

Alexander, C. (2010). *Tales of Glass Town, Angria, and Gondal: Selected Early Writings*. Oxford: Oxford University Press.

Alexander, C. (2018, July 4). In Search of the Authorial Self: Branwell Brontë's Microcosmic World. *Journal of Juvenilia Studies* 1: 3–19. doi:10.29173/jjs126. ISSN 2561-8326

Alter, R. (2008). *The Five Books of Moses with Commentary*. New York: W.W. Norton.

Alvarez, A. (2011). "Which Violence and Whose Violence? Questions Arising in the Psychotherapy of Aggressive Children." In *Aggression: From Phantasy to Action*, ed. P. Williams. London: Karnac.

Atwood, M. (2002). "Duplicity: The Jekyll Hand, the Hyde Hand, and the Slippery Double." In *Negotiating with the Dead: A Writer on Writing*. Anchor Books.

Bach, S. (1985). *Narcissistic States and the Therapeutic Process*. New York: Jason Aronson.

Bakhtin, M.M. (1981). *The Dialogic Imagination*, ed. M. Holquist, trans. C. Emerson and M. Holquist. Austin, TX: University of Texas Press.

Balint, E. (1963). "On Being Empty of Oneself." In Balint, E. (1993). *Before I Was I: Psychoanalysis and the Imagination*, ed. J. Mitchell and M. Parsons. London: Free Association Books.

Balint, E. (1993). *Before I Was I: Psychoanalysis and the Imagination*, ed. J. Mitchell and M. Parsons. London: Free Association Books.

Balint, E. (1993). "Creative Life." In *Before I Was I: Psychoanalysis and the Imagination*, ed. J. Mitchell and M. Parsons, London: Free Association Books.

Balint, M. (1959). *Thrills and Regressions*. London: Hogarth Press.

Barker, J. (1994). *The Brontes*. London: Weidenfeld & Nicolson.

Barker, J. (1997). *The Brontës: A Life in Letters*. New York: Overlook Press.

Barron, S., Draguet, M., and Tashjiian, D. (2006). *Magritte and Contemporary Art: The Treachery of Images*. Ludion/Los Angeles County Museum of Art.

Barth, J.R. (1977). *The Symbolic Imagination: Coleridge and the Romantic Tradition*. Princeton, NJ, Princeton University Press.

Bashō, M. (1966). *The Narrow Road to the Deep North and Other Travel Sketches*. London: Penguin.

Baudry, F. (2009). Winnicott's 1968 Visit to the New York Psychoanalytic Society and Institute: A Contextual View. *Psychoanalytic Quarterly* 78: 1059–90

Beehler, B. (2022). Charolette Brontë's Paper Dolls. *ELH Journal* 89 (1, Spring). https://muse.jhu.edu/article/848857

Beer, G. (1983). *Darwin's Plots: Evolutionary Narrative in Darwin, George Eliot and Nineteenth Century Fiction.* London: Routledge & Kegan Paul.

Bell, D. (2016). "The World as It Is vs the World as I Would Like It to Be." In *On Freud's "Formulations of Two Principles of Mental Functioning,"* ed. G. Legaretta and L. Brown. London and New York: Routledge, pp. 39–64.

Bentley, P.E. (1969). *The Brontes and Their World.* London: Thames & Hudson.

Bion, W. (1962). *Learning from Experience.* Lanham, MD: Rowman & Littlefield.

Bion, W.R. (1962). The Psycho-Analytic Study of Thinking. *International Journal of Psychoanalysis* 43: 306–10.

Bion, W.R. (1963) *Elements of Psycho-Analysis.* Psychoanalytic Electronic Publishing version. 4: 98–104.

Bion, W.R. (1967). "A Theory of Thinking." In *Selected Papers on Psycho-Analysis.* New York: Jason Aronson.

Bion, W.R. (1970). *Attention and Interpretation.* London: Maresfield Library.

Bishop, E. (2006). "Writing Poetry Is an Unnatural Act …" In *Edgar Allan Poe & the Juke-Box: Uncollected Poems, Drafts, and Fragments.* New York: Farrar, Straus & Giroux, pp. 207–15.

Blackmur, R.P. (1935). "Statements and Idyls, a Review of Norman Macleod's, 'Horizons of Death,'" *Poetry*, Vol XLVI, May,1935, p. 108.

Blechner, M. (2018). *The Mindbrain and Dreams.* London and New York: Routledge

Blom, M.A. (1975). Apprenticeship in "The World Below": Charlotte Brontë's *Juvenilia. ESC: English Studies in Canada* 1 (3): 290–303. Project MUSE. doi.org/10.1353/esc.1975.0028

Borges, J.L. (1964). "Borges and I." In *Labyrinths: Selected Stories & Other Writings.* New York: New Directions, pp. 246–7.

Boswell, R. (2008). *The Half-Known World: On Writing Fiction.* Minneapolis, MN. Graywolf Press.

Bowen, J., and Dinsdale, A. (n.d.). The Brontës' Early Writings: Combining Phantasy and Fact. British Library Video. www.YouTube.com/watch?v=0Z01Bzs0Dqo

Bowie, M. (1993). *Psychoanalysis and the Future of Theory.* Oxford and Cambridge, MA: Blackwell.

Brann, E. (1991). *The World of the Imagination.* Rowman & Littlefield.

Breton, A. (1924). Manifesto of Surrealism. www2.hawaii.edu/~freeman/courses/phil330/MANIFESTO OF SURREALISM.pdf

Brodsky, J. (1979). "Less Than One." *New York Review of Books*, September 27, 1979.

Bromberg, P. (1998). *Standing in the Spaces: Essays on Clinical Process, Trauma, and Dissociation.* Hillsdale, NJ: The Analytic Press.

Brontë, C. (1830). The Poetaster: A Drama by Lord Charles Wellesley, Charlotte Brontë, Relating to the Young Men, Play in Two Volumes [Haworth]: Autograph Manuscript Signed, 1830 June 8–July 12. Morgan Library, Literary and Historical Manuscripts (LHMS). http://corsair.themorgan.org/vwebv/holdingsInfo?bibId=81845

Brooks, P. (1994). *Psychoanalysis as Storytelling.* Cambridge, MA: Blackwell.

Brooks, P. (2022). *Seduced by Story: The Use and Abuse of Narrative.* New York: The New York Review of Books.

Bruner, J. (1987). Life as Narrative. *Social Research* 54 (1): 11–32.

Bruner, J. (1994). "The 'Remembered' Self." In *The Remembering Self: Construction and Accuracy in the Self-Narrative*, ed. U. Neisser and R. Fivush. Cambridge University Press.

Caldwell, L. (2000). *Art, Creativity and Living*. London: Karnac.

Caruth, C. (ed.). (1995). *Trauma: Explorations in Memory*. Baltimore and London: Johns Hopkins University Press.

Caruth, C. (2016). *Unclaimed Experience: Trauma, Narrative, and History*. Baltimore and London: Johns Hopkins University Press.

Castoriadis, C. (1997). *World in Fragments: Writings on Politics, Society, Psychoanalysis, and Imagination*. Stanford University Press.

Chao, S.-l. (2010). *Rethinking the Concept of the Grotesque: Crashaw, Baudelaire, Magritte*. London: Legenda.

Cohen, B. (2013). "The Dissociative Reality." In *Handbook of Dissociation: Theoretical, Empirical, and Clinical Perspectives*, ed. L. Michelson and W.J. Ray. Springer Science and Business Media.

Coleridge, S.T. (1802). "Dejection: An Ode." In *The Complete Poems*, ed. W. Keach. London: Penguin, 1997.

Coleridge, S.T. (1817). *Biographia Literaria*, ed. J. Engell and W.J. Bate. Princeton, NJ: Princeton University Press, 1983.

Cook, J. (2017). *The Lion Man: An Ice Age Masterpiece*. www.britishmuseum.org/blog/lion-man-ice-age-masterpiece

Cross, C. (2019). *Heavier Than Heaven: The Biography of Kurt Cobain*. London: Hodder & Stoughton.

D'Agata, J. (2016). *The Making of the American Essay*. Minneapolis, MN: Graywolf Press.

Descola, P. (2013). *Beyond Nature and Culture*. Chicago: University of Chicago Press.

Dewey, J. (1934). *Art as Experience*. New York: Perigee Books.

DiResta, R. (2019). "Mediating Consent." Ribbonfarm: Constructions in Magical Thinking. www.ribbonfarm.com/2019/12/17/mediating-consent/

Donoghue, D. (1973). *Thieves of Fire*. London: Faber.

Du Maurier, D. (1961). *The Infernal World of Branwell Brontë*. Garden City, NY: Doubleday.

Eden, V. (2018). Life Remains on the Surface of Silence: Lea Goldberg's Last Poems. *World Literature Today*. March 28. Online edition: www.worldliteraturetoday.org/blog/book-reviews/life-remains-surface-silence-lea-goldbergs-last-poems-vivian-eden

Ehrenzweig, A. (1971). *The Hidden Order of Art*. Berkeley and Los Angeles: University of California Press.

Eliot, G. (1990). "The Natural History of German Life." In George Eliot, *Selected Essays, Poems, and Other Writings*. London: Penguin Classics.

Eliot, T.S. (1922). *The Waste-Land*. www.poetryfoundation.org/poems/47311/the-waste-land

Eliot, T.S. (2023). "Burnt Norton." In *Four Quartets: A Poem*. Ecco.

Elkins, J. (2015). Motility, Aggression, and the Bodily I: An Interpretation of Winnicott. *The Psychoanalytic Quarterly* LXXXIV (4): 943–73.

Ellmann, R. (1982). *James Joyce*. London: Oxford University Press.

Emerson, R.W. (1841). Circles. https://emersoncentral.com/texts/essays-first-series/circles/

Erikson, E. (1977). *Toys and Reasons: Stages in the Ritualization of Experience*. New York: W.W. Norton.

Fassin, D. (2007). *When Bodies Remember: Experiences and Politics of AIDS in South Africa*. Oakland: University of California Press.

Fast, I. (2012). The Primary Processes Grow Up: Freud's More Radical View of the Mind. *Contemporary Psychoanalysis* 48 (2): 183–98.

Ferutta, A. (2019). Winnicott's Research on "Becoming" in Personal Psychic Life: "My Latest Brain-Child." *The Italian Psychoanalytic Annual* (13): 117–26.

Fonagy, P., Gergely, G., Jurist, E.L., and Target, M. (2002). *Affect Regulation, Mentalization, and the Development of the Self.* New York: Other Press.

Fonagy, P., and Target, M. (1996). Playing With Reality: I. Theory of Mind and the Normal Development of Psychic Reality. *International Journal of Psychoanalysis* 77: 217–33.

Fox, S. (1981). *John Muir and His Legacy.* Boston: Little, Brown.

Freud, S. (1892). [Notes I] from Extract from the Fliess Papers. In *The Standard Edition of the Complete Psychological Works of Sigmund Freud*, II: 248–50.

Freud, S. (1897). Letter 61 from "Extract from the Fliess Papers." In *The Standard Edition of the Complete Psychological Works of Sigmund Freud*, I: 247–8.

Freud, S. (1899). "Screen Memories." In *The Standard Edition of the Complete Psychological Works of Sigmund Freud*, III: 299–322.

Freud, S. (1905). "Three Essays on the Theory of Sexuality." In *The Standard Edition of the Complete Psychological Works of Sigmund Freud*, VII: 123–246.

Freud, S. (1906). "Creative Writers and Day-Dreaming." In *The Standard Edition of the Complete Psychological Works of Sigmund Freud*, IX, pp. 141–52.

Freud, S. (1911). "Formulations on the Two Principles of Mental Functioning." In *The Standard Edition of the Complete Psychological Works of Sigmund Freud*, XII: 213–26.

Freud, S. (1913 [1912–1913]). "Totem and Taboo: Some Points of Agreement Between the Mental Lives of Savages and Neurotics." In *The Standard Edition of the Complete Psychological Works of Sigmund Freud*, XIII: vii–162.

Freud, S. (1914). "Remembering, Repeating, and Working Through." In *The Standard Edition of the Complete Psychological Works of Sigmund Freud*, XII: 145–56.

Freud, S. (1917). "Introductory Lectures on Psycho-Analysis, Lecture XXIII: The Paths to the Formation of Symptoms." In *The Standard Edition of the Complete Psychological Works of Sigmund Freud*, XVI: 357–76.

Freud, S. (1917). "Mourning and Melancholia." In *The Standard Edition of the Complete Psychological Works of Sigmund Freud*, XIV: 237–58.

Freud, S. (1918). Letter from Sigmund Freud to Oskar Pfister, October 9, 1918. *Psychoanalysis and Faith: The Letters of Sigmund Freud and Oskar Pfister*, 59: 61–3. Psychoanalytic Electronic Publishing.

Freud, S. (1920). "Beyond the Pleasure Principle." In *The Standard Edition of the Complete Psychological Works of Sigmund Freud*, XVIII: 1–64.

Freud, S. (1923). "The Ego and the Id." In *The Standard Edition of the Complete Psychological Works of Sigmund Freud*, XIX, pp. 1–67.

Freud, S. (1926). "Inhibitions, Symptoms, and Anxiety." In *The Standard Edition of the Complete Psychological Works of Sigmund Freud*, XX: 77–178.

Freud, S. (1930). "Civilization and its Discontents." In *The Standard Edition of the Complete Psychological Works of Sigmund Freud*, XXI: 57–146

Freud, S. (1933). "New Introductory Lectures on Psycho-Analysis." In *The Standard Edition of the Complete Psychological Works of Sigmund Freud*, XXII: 1–182.

Freud, S. (1937). "Constructions in Analysis." In *The Standard Edition of the Complete Psychological Works of Sigmund Freud*, XXIII: 255–70.

Freud, S. (1938). "Findings, Ideas, Problems." In *The Standard Edition of the Complete Psychological Works of Sigmund Freud* XXIII: 299–300.

Frith, C. (2007). *Making Up the Mind: How the Brain Creates Our Mental World.* Malden, MA: Blackwell Publishing.

Fromm, E. (1991). *You Shall Be As Gods*. New York: Henry Holt.

Frost, R. (1930). "Education by Poetry." In *Robert Frost: Collected Poems, Prose and Plays*, ed. R. Poirier and M. Richardson. New York: Library of America, 1995, pp. 717–28.

Frye, N. (1969). *The Anatomy of Criticism*. New York: Atheneum.

Gérin, W. (1971). *Emily Brontë*. Oxford: Clarendon Press.

Gilbert, S., and Ellman, R. (eds.). (1966). *Letters of James Joyce*, Vol. 1. New York: The Viking Press.

Goldman, D. (1993). *In Search of the Real: The Origins and Originality of D.W. Winnicott*. Northvale, NJ: Jason Aronson.

Goldman, D. (2017). A Beholder's Share: essays on Winnicott and the psychoanalytic imagination. London and New York: Routledge.

Gombrich, E.H. (1960). *Art and Illusion: A Study in the Psychology of Pictorial Representation*. New York: Pantheon Books.

Gopnik, A. (2002, September 30). Bumping Into Mr. Ravioli. *The New Yorker*, 78 (29): 80.

Gopnik, A. (2009). *The Philosophical Baby: What Children's Minds Tell Us About Truth, Love, and the Meaning of Life*. New York: Picador.

Gussow, M. (2000). "Interview with Yehuda Amichai." *New York Times*, September 23, p. A14.

Harari, Y. (2015). *Sapiens: A Brief History of Humankind*. New York: HarperCollins.

Harman, C. (2017). *Charlotte Brontë: A Fiery Heart*. New York: Vintage Books.

Harris, P. (2000). *The Work of Imagination: Understanding Children's Worlds*. Oxford: Blackwell.

Hatfield, C.W. (ed.). (1941). *The Complete Poems of Emily Jane Brontë*. New York: Columbia University Press.

Healy, D. (1996). *The Bend for Home*. London: Harvill Press.

Horowitz, M. (1972). Modes of Representation of Thought. *Journal of the American Psychoanalytic Association* 20: 793–819.

Huizinga, J. (2016). *Homo Ludens: A Study of the Play Element in Culture*. Kettering, OH: Angelico Press.

Hutchins, P. (1957). *James Joyce's World*. North Yorkshire: Methuen.

James, H. (1879). Letter to William James. February 23, 1879. Houghton Library, Harvard University.

Joyce, J. (2022). *Portrait of an Artist as a Young Man*. Ottawa, Canada: East India Publishing.

Kandel, E. (2012). *Age of Insight: The Quest to Understand the Unconscious in Art, Mind, and Brain*. New York: Random House.

Kearney, R. (1988). *The Wake of Imagination*. Minneapolis, MN: University of Minnesota Press.

Kearney, R. (2002). *On Stories*. London: Routledge.

Keller, H., Otto, H., Lamm, B., Yovsi, R.D., and Kärtner, J. (2008). "The Timing of Verbal/ Vocal Communications Between Mothers and Their Infants: A Longitudinal Cross-Cultural Comparison." *Infant Behavior & Development* 31 (2): 217–26.

Lacan, J. (1997). *Écrits: A Selection*. London: Routledge.

Laing, R.D. (1969). *Self and Others*. London: Tavistock.

Lakoff, G., and Johnson, M. (1999). *Philosophy in the Flesh: The Embodied Mind and Its Challenge to Western Thought*. New York: Basic Books.

Lane, M. (1980). *The Drug-Like Brontë Dream*. London: John Murray.

Langer, S. (1942). *Philosophy in a New Key*. Cambridge, MA: Harvard University Press.

Langer, S. (1953). *Feeling and Form*. London: Routledge & Kegan Paul.

Lanzmann, C. (1995). "The Obscenity of Understanding: An Evening With Claude Lanzmann." In *Trauma: Explorations in Memory*, ed. C. Caruth. Baltimore and London: Johns Hopkins University Press, p. 204.

Laplanche, J. and Ponytails, J.B. (1973). *The Language of Psycho-Analysis*. New York: W.W. Norton.

Lear, J. (1996). The Introduction of Eros: Reflections on the Work of Hans Loewald. *Journal of the American Psychoanalytic Association* 44: 673–98.

Lee, H. (2003). "No She Said No." Review of "Lucia Joyce: To Dance in the Wake," by Carol Loeb Shloss. *New York Times Book Review*, December 28. www.nytimes.com/2003/12/28/books/no-she-said-no.html

Le Guin, U. (2011). "It Doesn't Have to Be the Way It Is." In *No Time to Spare: Thinking About What Matters*. Boston and New York: Houghton Mifflin Harcourt, 2017, p. 80.

Levine, G. (1988). *Darwin and the Novelists: Patterns of Science in Victorian Fiction*. Cambridge, MA: Harvard University Press.

Levine, H.B., Reed, G.S., and Scarfone, D. (2013). *Unrepresented States and the Construction of Meaning: Clinical and Theoretical Contributions*. London: Karnac Books.

Lewis, M. (2016). *The Undoing Project: A Friendship That Changed Our Minds*. W.W. Norton. Kindle edition.

Lifton, R.J. (2019). *Losing Reality: On Cults, Cultism, and the Mindset of Political and Religious Zealotry*. New York and London: The New Press. Kindle edition.

Loewald, H. (1971). "The Id and Regulatory Principles of Mental Functioning: A Discussion." In *Papers on Psychoanalysis*. New Haven: Yale University Press, 1980, pp. 58–68.

Loewald, H. (1978). *Papers on Psychoanalysis*. New Haven, CT: Yale University Press, 1980.

Loewald, H. (1978). "Primary Process, Secondary Process, and Language." In *Papers on Psychoanalysis*. New Haven: Yale University Press, 1980, pp. 178–206.

Lyons-Ruth, K. (2000). I Sense That You Sense That I SENSE: Sander's Recognition Process and the Specificity of Relational Moves in the Psychotherapeutic Setting. *Infant Mental Health Journal* 21 (1–2): 85–98.

MacGregor, N. "Living with the Gods" (2017, October 23). BBC Radio 4 Series, *The Beginnings of Belief*. Retrieved April 9, 2023. www.bbc.co.uk/sounds/play/b099xhmj

MacIntyre, A. (1981). *After Virtue: A Study in Moral Theory*. University of Notre Dame Press. First edition.

Magritte, René (2016). *René Magritte: Selected Writings*, ed. K. Rooney and E. Plattner. Minneapolis, MN: University of Minnesota Press.

Makin, S. (2020). "Born Ready: Babies Are Prewired to Perceive the World," *Scientific American*, March 2, 2020, www.scientificamerican.com/article/born-ready-babies-are-prewired-to-perceive-the-world/

Margaritoff, M. (2023). Inside the Text of Kurt Cobain's Heart Wrenching Suicide Note. *All That's Interesting* (ATI). June 4. https://allthatsinteresting.com/kurt-cobain-suicide-note

Marsden, S. (2014). *Emily Brontë and the Religious Imagination*. London: Bloomsbury.

McGilchrist, I. (2009). *The Master and his Emissary: The Divided Brain and the Making of the Western World*. New Haven, CT: Yale University Press.

Menand, L. (2012). Silence, Exile, Punning: James Joyce's Chance Encounters. *The New Yorker*, June 25. www.newyorker.com/magazine/2012/07/02/silence-exile-punning

Milner, M. (1952). Aspects of Symbolism in Comprehension of the Not-Self. *International Journal of Psychoanalysis* 33: 181–94.

Morrison, D., and Morrison, S.L. (2006). *Memories of Loss and Dreams of Perfection: Unsuccessful Childhood Grieving and Adult Creativity.* Amityville, NY: Baywood.

Muller, J.P., and Richardson, W.J. (1982). *Lacan and Language: A Reader's Guide to Écrits.* New York: International Universities Press.

Murdoch, I. (2014). *The Sovereignty of Good.* London and New York: Routledge.

Nin, A. (1961). *Seduction of the Minotaur.* Chicago: The Swallow Press.

O'Connor, F. (1988). *The Habit of Being: Letters of Flannery O'Connor.* New York: Farrar, Straus & Giroux.

Ogden, T. (2010). On Three Forms of Thinking. *Psychoanalytic Quarterly* LXXIX(2): 317–47.

Oliver, M. (1986). "Wild Geese." In *Dream Work.* New York: Grove/Atlantic, p. 347.

Phillips, A. (1994). *On Flirtation: Psychoanalytic Essays on the Uncommitted Life.* Cambridge, MA: Harvard University Press.

Phillips, J., and Morley, J. (2003). *Imagination and Its Pathologies.* Cambridge, MA: MIT Press.

Piers, M.W. (ed.). (1972). *Play and Development: A Symposium.* New York: Norton.

Plato. (1988). *The Laws of Plato,* trans. Thomas L. Pangle. Chicago: University of Chicago Press, 1st edition.

Poe, E.A. (1848). *The Complete Tales and Poems of Edgar Allan Poe.* New York: Barnes & Noble, 1992.

Pruyser, P. (1983). *The Play of Imagination: Toward a Psychoanalysis of Culture.* New York: International University Press.

Quinodoz, D. (2003). Words That Touch. *International Journal of Psychoanalysis* 84(6): 1469–85.

Ratchford, F.E. (1949). *The Brontës Web of Childhood.* New York: Columbia University Press.

Reis, B. (In Press). Freud's Animality. *International Journal of Psychoanalysis.*

Richards, I.A. (1969). *Coleridge on Imagination.* Bloomington, IN: Indiana University Press.

Robinson, G., and Rundell, J. (1994). *Rethinking Imagination: Culture and Creativity.* London and New York: Routledge.

Rodman, F. (2003). *Winnicott: Life and Work.* New York: Perseus Books.

Root-Bernstein, M. (2014). *Inventing Imaginary Worlds: From Childhood Play to Adult Creativity Across the Arts and Sciences.* Roman & Littlefield.

Roussillon, R. (2013). "The Deconstruction of Primary Narcissism." In *Donald Winnicott Today,* ed. J. Abram. London and New York: Routledge.

Rycroft, C. (1968). *Imagination and Reality.* New York: International Universities Press.

Sagan, C. (1995). *The Demon-Haunted World: Science as a Candle in the Dark.* New York: Random House.

Sandburg, C. (1916). *Chicago Poems.* New York: Henry Holt. (and Stilwell, KS: Digireads. com Publishing, p. 36.)

Sander, L. (1992). "Recognition Process: Organization and Specificity in Early Development: A Perspective on Developmental Process. Morton Levitt Memorial Lecture, University of California, Davis, April 21.

Santayana, G. (1989). *Interpretations of Poetry and Religion.* Cambridge, MA: MIT Press.

Santayana, G. (2011). *The Life of Reason, Introduction and Reason in Common Sense.* Cambridge, MA: MIT Press.

Segal, H. (1957). Notes on Symbol Formation. *International Journal of Psychoanalysis* 38: 391–7.

Shakespeare, W. (1969). *A Midsummer Night's Dream*. In *The Complete Pelican Shakespeare*. London: Penguin.

Sharpe, E.F. (1940). Psycho-Physical Problems Revealed in Language: An Examination of Metaphor. *International Journal of Psychoanalysis* 21: 201–13.

Shepard, O. (ed.) (1961). *The Heart of Thoreau's Journals*. New York: Dover.

Silvey, R., and MacKeith, S. (1988). "The Paracosm: A Special form of Phantasy." In *Organizing Early Experience: Imagination and Cognition in Childhood*, ed. D. Morrison. Amityville, NY: Baywood, pp. 173–97.

Simon, P. (1973). "Kodachrome." www.paulsimon.com/track/kodachrome-7/

Sodre, I. (1998). "Death by Daydreaming." In *Psychoanalysis and Culture: A Kleinian Perspective*, ed. D. Bell. Tavistock/Duckworth: Tavistock Clinic Series, 1998.

Sontag, S. (1975). "Fascinating Fascism." *New York Review of Books*, February 6.

Sontag, S. (1986). "Notes on 'Camp.'" In *Against Interpretation and Other Essays*. Picador Press, 2001, pp. 275–92.

Spence, D.P. (1982). *Narrative Truth and Historical Truth: Meaning and Interpretation in Psychoanalysis*. New York: W.W. Norton.

Spender, S. (1957). The Daytime World of James Joyce. *New York Times Books*, May 26. https://archive.nytimes.com/www.nytimes.com/books/00/01/09/specials/joyce-lett ers.html

Stern, D.B. (2003). *Unformulated Experience: From Dissociation to Imagination in Psychoanalysis*. London and New York: Routledge.

Stern, D.N. (1985). *The Interpersonal World of the Infant*. New York: Basic Books.

Stern, D.N. (2004). *The Present Moment in Psychotherapy and Everyday Life*. New York: W.W. Norton.

Stevens, M., and Swan, A. (2004). *de Kooning: An American Master*. New York: Knopf

Stevens, W. (1990). "Holiday in Reality." In *The Collected Poems of Wallace Stevens*. U.S. Vintage reissue edition.

Stoeri, J. (2005). Surprise, Shock, and Dread, and the Nature of Therapeutic Action. *Contemporary Psychoanalysis* 41: 183–202.

Strawson, G. (2018). *Things That Bother Me: Death, Freedom, the Self, etc.* New York: New York Review Books, Kindle edition.

Taipale, J. (2021). Being Carried Away. Fink and Winnicott on the Locus of Playing. *Journal of Phenomenological Psychology* 52: 193–217.

Taylor, C. (1989). *Sources of the Self*. Cambridge University Press.

Taylor, C. (2004). *Modern Social Imaginaries*. Duke University Press.

Taylor, M. (1999). *Imaginary Companions and the Children Who Create Them*. New York: Oxford University Press.

Tedeschi, J., and Tedeschi, A. (1990). "Clues: Roots of an Evidential Paradigm." In *Myths, Emblems, and the Historical Method*. Baltimore: Johns Hopkins University Press.

Tennyson, A. (1850). "In Memoriam A.H.H." www.online-literature.com/tennyson/718/

Thompson, J.B. (1985). *Studies in the Theory of Ideology*. Berkeley, CA: University of California Press.

van den Kolk, B. (2015). *The Body Keeps the Score: Brain, Mind, and Body in the Healing of Trauma*. Penguin.

Vivona, J. (2003). Embracing Figures of Speech. *Psychoanalytic Psychology* 20 (1): 52–66.

Vivona, J. (2006). From Developmental Metaphor to Developmental Model: The Shrinking Role of Language in the Talking Cure. *Journal of the American Psychoanalytic Association* 54: 877–902.

Vygotsky, L.S. (1978). *Mind in Society: The Development of Higher Psychological Processes*. Cambridge, MA: Harvard University Press.

Warnock, M. (1978). *Imagination*. Berkeley, CA: University of California Press.

Wilbur, R. (2004). *Richard Wilbur: Collected Poems 1943–2004*. New York: Harcourt.

Winnicott, D.W. (1941). "The Observation of Infants in a Set Situation." In *Through Pediatrics to Psycho-Analysis*. London: Hogarth, 1975, pp. 52–69.

Winnicott, D.W. (1945). "Primitive Emotional Development." In *Through Paediatrics to Psycho-Analysis*. New York: Basic Books, 1975, pp. 145–56.

Winnicott, D.W. (1948). "Pediatrics and Psychiatry." In *Through Pediatrics to Psycho-Analysis*. London: Hogarth, 1975, pp. 157–73.

Winnicott, D.W. (1949). "Birth Memories, Birth Trauma, and Anxiety." In *Through Pediatrics to Psycho-Analysis*. London: Hogarth, 1975, pp. 174–93.

Winnicott, D.W. (1949). "Mind and Its Relation to the Psyche-Soma." In *Through Paediatrics to Psycho-Analysis*. New York: Basic Books, 1975, pp. 243–54.

Winnicott, D.W. (1950–55). "Aggression in Relation to Emotional Development." In *Through Pediatrics to Psycho-Analysis*. London: Hogarth, 1975, pp. 204–18.

Winnicott, D.W. (1952). "Psychosis and Child Care." In *Through Pediatrics to Psycho-Analysis*. London: Hogarth, 1975, pp. 219–28.

Winnicott, D.W. (1953). Transitional Objects and Transitional Phenomena: A Study of the First Not-Me Possession. *International Journal of Psychoanalysis* XXXIV (2): 89–97.

Winnicott, D.W. (1956). "Primary Maternal Preoccupation." In *Through Paediatrics to Psycho-Analysis*. New York: Basic Books, 1975, pp. 300–5.

Winnicott, D.W. (1960). "The Theory of Parent–Infant Relationship." In *The Collected Works of D.W. Winnicott: Vol 6: 1960–1963*, ed. L. Caldwell and H. Taylor Robinson. Oxford: Oxford University Press, pp. 141–58.

Winnicott, D.W. (1963). "D.W.W's Dream Related to Reviewing Jung." In *Psychoanalytic Explorations*. Cambridge, MA: Harvard University Press, pp. 228–30.

Winnicott, D.W. (1964). "Roots of Aggression." In *The Child, the Family, and the Outside World*. Harmondsworth, UK: Penguin, pp. 232–9.

Winnicott, D.W. (1964). "The Baby as a Going Concern." In *The Child, the Family, and the Outside World*. Harmondsworth: Penguin, 25–9.

Winnicott, D.W. (1964). "Why Children Play." In *The Child, the Family, and the Outside World*. Harmondsworth, UK: Penguin, pp. 134–8.

Winnicott, D.W. (1965). "Communicating and Not Communicating Leading to a Study of Certain Opposites." In *The Maturational Process and the Facilitating Environment*. London: Hogarth.

Winnicott, D.W. (1965). "New Light on Children's Thinking." In *Psychoanalytic Explorations*. Cambridge, MA: Harvard University Press, pp. 152–7.

Winnicott, D.W. (1967). "Postscript: D.W.W. on D.W.W." In *Psychoanalytic Explorations*. Cambridge, MA: Harvard University Press, pp. 569–82.

Winnicott, D.W. (1968). "Communication Between Mother and Infant and Infant and Mother, Compared and Contrasted." In *Babies and Their Mothers*, ed. C. Winnicott, R. Shepherd, and M. Davis. Reading, MA: Addison-Wesley, 1987.

Winnicott, D.W. (1969). "The Pill and the Moon." In *Home Is Where We Start From: Essays by a Psychoanalyst*, ed. C. Winnicott, R. Shepherd, and M. Davis. New York: W.W. Norton, 1986, pp. 195–209.

Winnicott, D.W. (1969). The Use of an Object. *International Journal of Psychoanalysis.* 50: 711–16.

Winnicott, D.W. (1969). "The Use of an Object in the Context of Moses and Monotheism." In *Psychoanalytic Explorations.* Cambridge, MA: Harvard University Press, 1989, pp. 240–6.

Winnicott, D.W. (1970). "Individuation." In *Psychoanalytic Explorations.* Cambridge, MA: Harvard University Press, 1989, pp. 284–88.

Winnicott, D.W. (1971). "Creativity and Its Origins." In *Playing and Reality.* Tavistock, pp. 65–85.

Winnicott, D.W. (1971). *Playing and Reality.* Tavistock.

Winnicott, D.W. (1971). "Playing: Creative Activity and the Search for the Self." In *Playing and Reality.* Tavistock, pp. 53–64.

Winnicott, D.W. (1971). "The Place Where We Live." In *Playing and Reality.* Tavistock, pp. 104–10.

Winnicott, D.W. (1974). Fear of Breakdown. *International Review of Psychoanalysis* 1: 103–7.

Winnicott, D.W. (1986). *Home Is Where We Start From: Essays by a Psychoanalyst,* ed. C. Winnicott, R. Shepherd, and M. Davis. New York: Norton.

Winnicott, D.W. (1988). *Human Nature.* New York: Schocken Books.

Wittgenstein, L., and Rhees, R. (1968). Conversations on Freud. *Psychoanalytic Review* 55: 376–86.

Wood, J. (2015). *The Nearest Thing to Life.* Brandeis University Press.

Woolf, V. (1928). *Orlando: A Biography.* Kindle version.

Woolf, V. (1985). "A Sketch of the Past." In *Moments of Being.* San Diego, New York, and London: A Harvest Book, Harcourt, pp. 61–160.

Wordsworth, W. (1798). "Essay on Morals." In *The Prose Works of William Wordsworth,* ed. W.J.B. Owen and J.W. Smyser. London: Oxford University Press, 1974.

Wordsworth, W. (1798). "Lines Written a Few Miles Above Tintern Abbey." In *William Wordsworth: The Major Works, Including the Prelude,* ed. S. Gill. New York: Oxford University Press, 2008, pp. 131–5.

Wordsworth, W. (1805). "The Prelude." In *William Wordsworth: The Major Works,* ed. S. Gill. New York: Oxford University Press, 2008, pp. 375–590.

Wordsworth, W. (1996). *The Prelude.* Penguin Classics. Revised edition.

Wright, K. (1991). *Vision and Separation: Between Mother and Baby.* Northvale, NJ: Jason Aronson.

Wright, K. (2009). *Mirroring and Attunement: Self-Realization in Psychoanalysis and Art.* Hove, UK: Routledge.

Yeats, W.B. (1933). "A Prayer for Old Age." https://allpoetry.com/A-Prayer-For-Old-Age

Young, K. (1930). "Language and Social Interaction." In *Social Psychology: An Analysis of Social Behavior.* New York: Alfred A. Knopf (1930), Chapter 10, 203–32.

Zalewski, D. (2009). "The Background Hum, Ian McEwan's Art of Unease." *The New Yorker,* February 23, 2009.

Index

For Product Safety Concerns and Information please contact our EU
representative GPSR@taylorandfrancis.com
Taylor & Francis Verlag GmbH, Kaufingerstraße 24, 80331 München, Germany

www.ingramcontent.com/pod-product-compliance
Lightning Source LLC
Chambersburg PA
CBHW052008270326
41929CB00015B/2838